Tejanaland

Women in Texas History Series
Sponsored by the Ruthe Winegarten Memorial Foundation
Nancy Baker Jones and Cynthia J. Beeman,
General Editors

The following individuals and organizations helped
make the publication of this series possible:
  Ellen C. Temple
  Leadership Women
  Texas Historical Foundation
  T. L. L. Temple Foundation
  Devorah Winegarten

Tejanaland

A Writing Life in Four Acts

Teresa Palomo Acosta

Foreword by Nancy Baker Jones
and Cynthia J. Beeman

Texas A&M University Press
College Station

This paper meets the requirements of ANSI/NISO Z39.48–1992
(Permanence of Paper).
Binding materials have been chosen for durability.
Manufactured in the United States of America

Library of Congress Cataloging-in-Publication Data

Names: Acosta, Teresa Palomo, author. | Jones, Nancy Baker, writer of
  foreword. | Beeman, Cynthia J., writer of foreword.
Title: Tejanaland: a writing life in four acts / Teresa Palomo Acosta;
  foreword by Nancy Baker Jones and Cynthia J. Beeman.
Other titles: Women in Texas history series.
Description: First edition. | College Station: Texas A&M University Press,
  [2021] | Series: Women in Texas history series
Identifiers: LCCN 2021019290 | ISBN 9781623499884 (cloth) | ISBN
  9781623499891 (ebook)
Subjects: LCSH: Acosta, Teresa Palomo. | Mexican American women
  authors—Texas—Biography. | Mexican American women—Texas—Social
  conditions. | Mexican American women—Texas—Social conditions—Poetry.
  | Mexican American women—Texas—Social conditions—Drama. | Hispanic
  American mothers—Texas—Juvenile fiction. | Mexican American
  women—Texas—Ethnic identity. | Self in literature. | Feminism and
  literature. | LCGFT: Autobiographical fiction. | Autobiographical drama.
  | Autobiographical poetry. | Creative nonfiction.
Classification: LCC PS3551.C62 T45 2021 | DDC 810.8/092870896872—dc23
LC record available at https://lccn.loc.gov/2021019290

Contents

A gallery of images follows page 50.

Foreword

Teresa Palomo Acosta's *Tejanaland* marks another new turn for the Women in Texas History book series. History for some is a straightforward, footnoted account of the past constructed at a remove by a trained historian. But more accurately, perhaps, it is simply human experience, recorded. Memoir is a form of history, and biographical literary creations are a form of memoir. In this work we have a collection of plays, essays, and poems created from the grist of the author's life and assembled in chronological order from 1988 to 2018.

As Gerda Lerner, one of the founders of women's history, wrote decades ago, the true history of women is the story of their existence written on their own terms, from their own perspectives and experiences. Their resources may be those traditionally used by professional historians, but they also bring to the fore their own documents, like letters, diaries, oral histories, and autobiographies that are not only essays, but also poems, plays, and fiction. Historical evidence comes in many forms, and women have for a long time expanded and broken the boundaries that have constrained how history is defined.

New voices push against traditional pathways to record their experiences and memories. Why not?

Texas A&M University Press has had a role in pushing boundaries such as these. It published *Life Along the Border*, the 1929 MA thesis of Jovita González, who became a renowned folklorist and author of an historical novel that is recognized not only as literature but also for its early use of ethnic and gender conflicts in Texas history. In addition, the press republished Elena Zamora O'Shea's classic 1935 novella, *El Mesquite*, in which the author favored local and family histories over official archives to tell the story of the region between the Nueces and Rio Grande through the persona of a Mesquite tree. In 2001, TAMU Press also published Historia: *The Literary Making of Chicana and Chicano History*, by Louis Mendoza, which was noted for making "a superb contribution to the multidisciplinary exploration of ways Mexican Americans have chosen to present their past through both 'factual' and 'fictional' narratives. . . . By juxtaposing the literary and the historical, he provides new insight on culture, agency, and experience." Among the writers Mendoza included was Teresa Palomo Acosta, who has published her own collections and whose work has been anthologized.

Tejanaland carries readers into the past through storytelling and remembrance, as she has said, to "a space called Central Texas, where I grew up. The plays particularly deal with art as discovered in a family's life—mine in particular—and a history of gun violence. The poems are an effort to expand out as a human being, something that too many in our publishing world still do not think Latinas have the right to do." These pieces, in their clarity, also expand our understanding of Tejana literary production during the period in which Acosta was writing. So they function both as history and artifact. Her poetry is quiet, moving, and expressive, drawing readers into contemplation as well as the author's self-revelation, and joining a procession of Tejanx creative writers like Jovita González de Mireles, Américo Paredes, Sara Estela Ramírez, and David Montejano, among others.

The Ruthe Winegarten Foundation for Texas Women's History is proud to have facilitated the publication of a volume that provides a unique and compelling look into the experiences and contemplations of a Texas artist worth knowing and that provides readers a way to increase their understanding of Tejana experience in the late 20th and early 21st centuries.

—Nancy Baker Jones and Cynthia J. Beeman
General Editors

Acknowledgments

Some materials in this book are from the Teresa Palomo Acosta Papers at the Nettie Lee Benson Latin American Collection, University of Texas Libraries, University of Texas at Austin.

Margo Gutiérrez and Carla Alvarez, librarian and archivist respectively with the Mexican American Collection at the Benson, deserve special mention. Margo helped me greatly over many years to establish the Teresa Palomo Acosta Papers. Carla has continued to assist in this capacity and provided for easy retrieval of materials I needed for this book.

Many other individuals and organizations have supported my work as a writer. Thank you for welcoming me into your homes, universities, and other public spaces to gain insights, share literature and history, and teach a new generation.

I thank the Ruthe Winegarten Memorial Foundation for Texas Women's History, and especially Nancy Baker Jones and Cynthia J. Beeman, for their interest in this book.

Chris Dodge, a gifted and meticulous copy editor, unquestionably enhanced my book. His gracious professionalism made our work together a felicitous journey.

For their caring support, I offer deep gratitude to my sister Olivia Acosta García, my brother Andrés Alderete Acosta Jr., and my late brother Jesse Palomo Acosta.

I send many *abrazos* and *gracias* to the holy trinity of Sabina Palomo Acosta and Andrés Alderete Acosta Sr., my parents, and to Maximino Palomo, my maternal grandfather. *Que en paz descansen.*

They answered my many questions and recounted to me story after story about who we were and what brought our family to McGregor, Texas. They set me on a path I would not otherwise have found.

Introduction

This book includes plays, a children's story, essays, and poems that cover three decades of my writing, from 1988 through 2018.

Each work addresses cultural, gender, historical, and political realities that I have experienced from my childhood to the present. I have not always willingly undertaken the challenges that have been set before me as a writer, except through poetry, the genre in which I find myself most completely at home.

The Plays

I wrote the theatrical works as part of a trilogy I undertook in 1988. Plays first appealed to me, when as a nineteen-year-old, I stumbled upon the works of Anton Chekhov and August Strindberg at a tiny bookstore in the basement of a clothing store blocks away from my job at an insurance company in downtown Waco, Texas. I had only read a tad of Shakespeare—via CliffsNotes, most likely in high school. The plays I found in that bookstore brought to me a world eloquently conveyed by characters and circumstances invented by playwrights. Chekhov's and Strindberg's plays were available in inexpensive paperback editions, so I plunked down money and took them with me. I devoured the works of these and other playwrights whose names I can no longer remember. I read some of the works over and again.

Both plays in this book are set in the Central Texas Blacklands of my upbringing. *Casa de Amor* (House of Love) explores how violence that erupts from socially accepted means affects one family. *Violin Playing* brings together drama and poetry. The play pays tribute to Maximino Palomo, my maternal grandfather. My grandfather did indeed play violin, and he insisted that I practice the soprano clarinet that I began to study as a sixth-grade student. The clarinet belonged to my sister Olivia.

The Children's Story

"Colchas, Colchitas" is an homage to my mother and to the many women of her generation who employed their needle and thread to create bed coverings from fabrics, thereby bringing beauty into our souls and keeping us warm in winter.

An editor from an East Coast publishing house who was based, as I recall, in San Antonio, asked me if I wrote children's stories. I told her that I did not. Nonetheless, I accepted her invitation to write one I titled "Colchas, Colchitas." The publisher ultimately rejected the piece. The work, loosely based on my poem "My Mother Pieced Quilts," disappeared into my writing bin. Years later, I made one hundred copies of a slightly different version that was illustrated by Mirta Toledo, an Argentinian artist with whom I have collaborated on various projects.

The Essays

I indulged in completely intentional heroine worship by writing about Jovita González de Mireles, Sara Estela Ramírez, and Elena Zamora O'Shea. Independently, and as a group, these Tejana writers wrote defining, excellent, and important work. In doing so, they contributed significantly to Tejano literature and to Texas letters. I consider all three of them my literary *abuelas*. I hope that my essays about them will encourage readers to explore their works, thereby embracing and upholding their accomplishments.

The essays about González de Mireles and Ramírez are drawn from formal papers I presented at historical gatherings; the piece about Zamora O'Shea is based on a talk I delivered. I wrote the fourth in response to a request by professor María Eugenia Cotera of the University of Michigan. She asked me to set down my thoughts regarding my experience in collaborating with the late historian Ruthe Winegarten on our 2003 book *Las Tejanas: 300 Years of History*. Writing this piece was a joy.

The Poems

The poems appear in the order that I wrote them between 2013 and 2018. These works convey my experiences with flowers, inward and outward journeys, and illness and recovery.

Poetry first found me as teenager. Poetry also found me as I read Mexican American history, as I learned about my family's stories, as I studied at the University of Texas at Austin, and as I joined fellow Chicana poets at the table of artistic and intellectual discourse.

My poems often come to me as I traverse a street, hear a comment with which I find myself in agreement or in opposition, and encounter nature, whether in trees, flowers, rocks, or something else. They all say to me, "I think there's something here you can document in writing."

Tejanaland

Act I
Plays

Casa de Amor (ca. 1980s)

Violin Playing (ca. 1980s)

Casa de Amor

A Play in Two Acts

Characters
Ana, 24
Gonzalo, 24, her husband
Dr. Carolina Suárez, 35
Juana, 56, Ana's aunt
Estebio, 56, Juana's husband
Sheriff Phillips, in his 60s

Settings: A bus, a grave, the family farmhouse, and the Good Samaritan
  Clinic in Central Texas
Time: When people were going to San Francisco, seeking love and peace
Circumstances: Ana is on a seemingly endless journey to find love and
  peace, a journey precipitated by the death of her five-year old son,
  Sebastian (Tati) Marcos, approximately one year ago. For the last
  twelve months she has wandered throughout the state supporting
  herself as a waitress and hotel maid. She returns home to settle some
  things regarding Tati's death.
A word on the characters and use of Spanish: All the characters are Mex-
  ican Americans except for the sheriff, who is white. All have various
  Central Texas drawls, from faint to strong. Some Spanish words and
  phrases, based on standard Spanish and Spanish dialects, are used
  throughout the play.

Act I
SCENE I

*Chairs resembling the seats of a bus are on one side of the stage. Tati's grave is
downstage and on the opposite side. Ana is wearing bell-bottom faded jeans, a
flowered shirt tied around her waist, a blue jean vest, moccasins, and love beads.*

She has a bandana tied around her forehead. A sparrow is tucked in her vest pocket. She carries a suitcase and a birdcage. As she enters the bus, she speaks and waves goodbye to someone offstage.

Ana: Don't worry about paying me. The uniform's yours to keep. (*Reaching into her vest to retrieve the sparrow.*) It's taking our last ten dollars in tips, Amorcito, to get us back to where we don't want to be. We're staying only the weekend. That's it. You hear that, Tati. I took my six hundred dollars and ran away from them and their guns and goat kicker dances. I knew what they were going to do after the funeral. Drink and take off on a deer hunting trip. Gonzalo took you, my Tati, my baby, along. "Don't do it!" I yelled. "If you take him, you're responsible for anything that goes wrong." (*Pause.*) You were gone by the time I made it to the Good Samaritan Clinic. Who killed you, Tati? Who? Whose gun? No one would say. Maybe Gonzalo's? Oh, it couldn't be. And Gonzalo says to me, you know what he says. He tells me this long drawn out story. He says . . .

Blackout

Gonzalo enters and stands near Tati's grave. He is wearing jeans, a plaid shirt, a cap, and work shoes. Ana is on the opposite side of Tati's grave.

Gonzalo: No one was gunning for Tati. It was just an awful accident. Nobody set him up for a hit. Rafael saw something out of the corner of his eye. "Another one, another!" He yells. And we scrambled for our guns. I thought Tati was in the truck. I put him there right before we started to load the deer. Somehow, he must have scrambled out and scampered away. Maybe he saw the same deer we did and was playing at catching it. Anyway, we grabbed our shotguns and took off. We followed for several feet. We spotted the deer's head in some bushes—all brown and grey—in the dark. One of us, I don't remember who, aimed and shot. It ducked out of sight at the last minute. We ran over, still hoping to get it. Then we saw something on the ground. It was Tati! It was Tati! I picked him up. We jumped into the truck. You know the rest.

Ana: You bet I do. Every minute I'm alive and breathing.

Black Out

SCENE II

Ana knocks on the door of a farmhouse. The living room is furnished with old and mismatched pieces. A velvet John F. Kennedy portrait decorates one wall and a couple of other inexpensive portraits of a deer and a bear hang on another. A gun rack with only one shotgun is next to the door. A TV is set on a rolling cabinet. Juana peers in from the kitchen [offstage] into the living room a second after she hears the door knock.

Juana: *A ver. A ver. ¿Quién es?*

Ana: Tía, it's me.

Juana (*opening the door*): Ana? Ah, *eres tú, mujercita.* It's been a while.

Ana (*enters with her suitcase and bird cage; Amorcito is perched on a shoulder*): I'm here for a couple of days. Heading to love, to music. To Frisco.

Juana: Does Gonzalo know you're here?

Ana: Uh, no. I checked at the gin. He was out at the Welch Ranch doing some work. Don't worry. I'll see him.

Juana: He's a dead man, Ana, since you left. ¡Que mala *fuiste con él!*

Ana (*angry, making a move to leave*): Nope, nope, I'm not going to leave just yet. Ya'll would love it if I took off again and was never heard from. Well, I'll get out of here by Sunday—not a day later. But first I want to leave some money for Tati's headstone. I've been saving for it. And I plan to talk to the sheriff again. See what's he come up with. See if I can press charges.

Juana: Ah, listen, Ana, leave it alone. Why do you want to dredge up the past?

Ana: Because it's still here inside me, *tía.*

Juana: He's buried. It was an accident. No one meant to hurt him.

Ana: That's supposed to take care of everything? Well, it doesn't. I want an answer to Tati's *muerte.*

Juana: You won't change anything with all your questions. No matter what you think. Nobody's talking any more. It's been a year. As far as we're concerned, God took Tati as an *angelito.*

Ana: An *angelito!* Not the God I know. He doesn't go around hunting deer and shooting children.

Juana: It's a mistake, Ana, to come back and make trouble.

Ana: What? You think I'm only here to raise your blood pressure?

Juana: I loved Tati!

Ana: Yep, you're right. You loved him. I loved him. We all loved him. But he's dead just the same.

Juana: Would have turned six this summer. And learned how to swim.

Ana: Would have started first grade.

Juana: Maybe even skipped it. He knew his numbers, liked to read. Smart. Real smart. Oh, God, Tati!

(Estebio enters. He goes over to the gun rack without noticing the women, pulls the gun down, and starts to load it.)

Estebio: *Vieja,* I'm going to find us a rabbit for our supper. If I'm lucky, I'll get a couple more for later.

Juana: Estebio, are you blind? Your niece is here.

Estebio: Huh? What? *(Looks up and stares at Ana.) Que bueno verte.* It's good to have you back. We thought about you all the time. Had your *tía* going crazy. No word from you. No idea if you were okay.

Juana: *Pues parece que se mira bien.*

Ana: Tío, I'm just passing through. I'll be gone Sunday.

Estebio: What? Just two days for the people who brought you up? Where you bound? Are you traveling all by yourself?

Juana: She's going to California. Where all those hippies we see on TV are smoking dope.

Ana: Now just a minute, *tía,* you don't know what I'll be doing.

Estebio: So, what else is going on out there?

Ana: Love.

Estebio: *¿Esa gente? ¿Qué saben esos del amor?* How about our love for you? Family love?

Ana: The kind that killed *m'ijo?* That love?

Estebio: We're not thugs, Ana. Out here we need to hunt our food. It's not a once-a-year game with us. We do it to find good game to eat. And we don't shoot *niños* on purpose. You need to get that through your hippie head. And what's that bird doing sitting on your shoulder? You're going to get a disease.

Ana: Maybe not you. Maybe you don't kill *niños.* But the others.

Juana: Blame. Blame. It's the same story as before. Maybe you shouldn't have come after all. To lay blame where there's none.

Estebio (*relenting a bit*): Oh, *vieja*, she lost her *hijo*. I'd already have caused a lot more trouble than you have, *m'ija*. I'd have shot me the son of a—

Ana: Look, this isn't about causing you trouble. And don't give me any baloney about needing to hunt to eat. You have chickens and hogs and cows and a garden. You only hunt to hunt. What'd a jackrabbit ever do to you to deserve to get thrown into your kettle?

Estebio (*suddenly angry*): Got in my way. I don't let 'em get in my way without bringing 'em down. I don't make 'em have to decide to get out of my way. (*Leaves, slamming the door.*)

Juana (*yelling after him*): Estebio!

Juana (to Ana): He's kidding. Estebio's been a hunter since he was a kid. And he's taught everyone else he could. Don't judge him. Your Tati was up next—with a BB gun first. If you'd have let him learn how to shoot.

Ana: And I never would.

Juana: Ah, *sí, yo se*. Come on into the kitchen. I need to finish mopping.

Ana: I can't. I need to get to the gin to talk to Gonzalo.

Juana: He'll come by if you ask. Call him.

Ana (*thinking it over*): Okay.

Juana: The number's 426—.

Ana (*dialing*): I know it, I know it.

Ana (*on the phone*): Gonzalo? It's me.

Blackout

SCENE III

Later that evening Estebio is settling down to watch his favorite TV game show when Gonzalo arrives. He taps on the door and comes in.

Gonzalo: *Tío. Buenas noches. ¿Cómo le va?*

Estebio (*places a bowl of popcorn on the sofa*): *Bien. Bien.*

Estebio (*yelling to his wife*): Hurry, *vieja*! It's about to start.

Juana (*offstage*): ¡Hay vengo! ¡Hay vengo!

Gonzalo: *Con perdón. Busco a Ana.* Is she around? She called a while ago.

Estebio: Yeah, she's here somewhere. *Vieja*, get Ana. *El* Gon is here.

Juana (*scurrying into the room in her usual harried fashion*): ¡Ana, te llama Gonzalo! M'ija, Gon's here! (*She offers him a chair and settles next to Estebio on the couch.*)

(*Ana rushes in but stops in her tracks when she sees Gonzalo, takes a deep breath.*)

Ana: Gonzalo. Uh—

Estebio (*clinging to the bowl of popcorn*): *Vieja*, let's roll the TV into the kitchen. You, two, straighten it out, okay?

Juana (*leaving with Estebio*): Look, Estebio, it's a new prize this time. A trip to Beverly Hills to see the homes of the stars. Got your game cards ready?

(*The sound of the closing kitchen door can be heard. Ana walks up to Gonzalo, then stops just short of him.*)

Gonzalo: Can you give me a kiss, *vieja*?

Ana: I'm not your *vieja*.

Gonzalo: Whose are you these days?

Ana: My own.

Gonzalo: Sounds lonely.

Ana: Yeah? Well, I can take it. It's half the work.

Gonzalo: Well, maybe. A man's handy to have around.

Ana (*changing tone*): I'm just back to find out what to do about Tati. I'm seeing the sheriff and that doctor—the one at the clinic, the one who held my hand while I waited that day. I'm seeing her tonight. Then I'm leaving again.

Ana (*suddenly very sad*): Oh, Gonzalo, I'm still waking up hoping that he's next door in his bed with his *colchita* wrapped and twisted around him, his socks off, as usual. It's been 369 days, and I still haven't said my good-byes to him. I wash dishes in restaurants and make up beds at hotels and talk to him all the time. "Tati, it's time to get up, it's time to have supper, it's time to play. Mami will read you a story. It's time to pick up Daddy." I walk up behind *niños* all the time, thinking that when they turn around, one of them will be Tati. My Tati.

Gonzalo (*trying to embrace her*): Ana, let's say good-bye to him together. Let's try it. Figure out how to.

Ana: I can't—just like that. He was our son, Gonzalo. And we lost him. From one second to the next.

Gonzalo: Look, *vieja*, I'm not a total jerk. I loved him too.

Ana: It won't work, Gonzalo. And please don't call me *vieja*. I've always hated that word.

Gonzalo: All right. Never again. I promise not to—even if you beg me.

Ana: I'm not joking. I'm Ana, not some *vieja* no one can see behind a man.

Gonzalo: Okay. Okay. "Ana" it is. I love your name. "Ana." "Ana." "Ana." See there, I can say it so easily.

Ana: Look, we must limit what we talk about to Tati. You and me, well, I can't. Tati's the reason for me to see you. You file the divorce papers. I'll get you an address in California for you to mail them to me to sign.

Gonzalo: Divorce papers! So *you're* calling all the shots.

Ana: When I left last year, that was it.

Gonzalo: No. No, it wasn't. It isn't.

Ana: You didn't hear me. I'm talking to Sheriff Phillips. To Dr. Suárez. And then I'm leaving. Only coming back for legal proceedings. Understand?

Gonzalo: You're not the only one who lost a son. I did too. I have rights. What do you mean by legal proceedings?

Ana: I bet you haven't done a thing about Tati since I left, have you. Not one thing.

Gonzalo: What have you done? With all your town hopping. Do you think I'm just a gun-toting nut? You married me, didn't you? Let me be Tati's father. I kept him fed. You fed. Clothed. (*Stopping to stare at her, taking in her clothing.*) The week after you vamoosed, I talked to Phillips, asked what I should do. "What do you want to do? What does Ana want to do?" he says. I could tell Tati was the last thing on his mind. You know how he is. Always some other biggie going on. A drunk or two to arrest. So I pestered him until he gave me an answer. I asked him, is there anything I can do, I should do? Do I turn myself in?' And he yells, "It was an accident! Who you going to charge? Yourself? Your wife's uncle? Your hunting buddies? The kid's dead and buried, and your wife's run off. You ought to go after her instead of trying to pin this on anyone. It could have been just about anybody. Did anybody fire first that you remember?" Well, he goes on and on like this for a while, and I'm trying to decide if it's worth all the pain.

Ana: Worth the pain? Tati got shot to death. You better believe it's worth it.

Gonzalo: Hold on. I know how dead he is. I've been to his grave every week for fifty-two weeks straight. Taking him flowers, talking to him like a crazy man. I— (*Putting up his hands when Ana tries to stop him.*) Listen, don't interrupt. I have cried, lit candles, prayed, burned my gun, stopped hunting, gone to confession, stopped drinking, stopped smoking, nearly stopped eating, stopped—

Ana: Everything, right? Stopped living, right? A saint staying behind, cleaning the grave, keeping it nice and tidy. I appreciate it, okay? But you didn't do a thing about why Tati's in his grave except to talk to the lazy sheriff about it, what, once? Everyone must think you're great. ¡Un santo! Not like his wife, the hippie. She ran off. Almost left Tati at the cemetery half-buried. Why didn't anybody want to take responsibility for what happened? I mean, somebody's to blame.

Gonzalo: But who can we blame?

Ana: My God, a lot of guys were there.

Gonzalo: Oh, yeah, sure, including me.

Ana: You took him with you. I said, "Don't do it." That was supposed to be our agreement.

Gonzalo: *Oye, amor.* I've used up all my answers. Come on, I'll take you to see Dr. Suárez.

Ana (*suddenly fearful*): You want to go with me? Maybe we *should* see her together.

Gonzalo (*hesitantly*): Sure, sure.

Blackout

SCENE IV

The Good Samaritan Clinic, where Dr. Suárez is in her office.

Dr. Suárez (*reading her notes aloud*): Mother, age twenty-three; father, age twenty-three. Married for seven years. Sebastian (Tati), their son. Age at death: five. Both parents refused to see any counselors at the clinic. Mother blames husband. Father very distraught, crying throughout the emergency room procedures carried out to try to save his son's life. Mother did not cry. Refused all tranquilizers. I tried to slip a note into her hand. She turned away.

Dr. Suárez (*responding to knock on door*): Ana—and Gonzalo—please come in. Please, have a seat. ¿Un café?

Gonzalo: No, *gracias.*

Dr. Suárez: *¿Cómo les puedo ayudar?*

Ana: *Doctora,* I don't know where to start. I'm not even sure I should be talking to you. Listen, I hope you don't mind that Gonzalo came with me.

Dr. Suárez: It's okay. You lost your son a year ago, right?

Ana: Well, no, it's been 369 days ago. I meant to get back right on the anniversary, but I had to work a few more days.

Dr. Suárez: Maybe we can figure out together what you want to talk about. What's bothering you, Ana? And you, Gonzalo?

Gonzalo: Well, we're just your everyday couple. We lost a son, and I'm responsible for his death. You might say that I killed him.

Dr. Suárez: How did you kill him?

Gonzalo: I took a five-year-old child, the only kid I'd willingly loved, on his final trip with Papi. I shook him awake on a cold morning, forced on his clothes, and strapped his toy gun to his jacket. I didn't even let him kiss his *mami* before we left. I packed him a candy bar and a soda pop. I forgot to bring his gloves along. I forgot to bring his fuzzies in case he wanted to sleep. I marched him out to the pickup and dumped him in the back with one of the other guys to hold down when we hit bumps in the road. I raced full speed ahead with the guys, the ammo, the beer, and a child, heading for a sure thing in the woods.

Dr. Suárez: For what sure thing?

Gonzalo: For Tati's death.

Dr. Suárez (*calmly*): Why were you going to Tati's death? Did you plan to go out there with the guys, line Tati against a tree, and shoot him?

Gonzalo: I might as well have. I mean, he ran right into a trap, didn't he? We were crazy drunk men even before the final blow, even before Tati—

Dr. Suárez: Did you tell the authorities that you were crazy drunk men?

Gonzalo: We, we, well, not me, I wasn't. But some of the guys had a lot to drink. Me, well, I'd had maybe two, three, but it takes a lot more to do me in. I've been a drinker from way back. But not a drop since Tati's death. Nothing. I swear.

Ana: Gonzalo, you do understand, don't you, that you loaded your gun the same as your buddies. Maybe we don't need Dr. Suárez. Maybe we, no, maybe I need to call the law.

Ana (*to Dr. Suárez*): *Doctora,* how about loaning me your phone to call Sherriff Phillips and see if he or one of his deputies can get up out of their easy boy chairs and manage to take Gonzalo in for questioning. How about it, *doctora?*

Dr. Suárez: Ana, you cannot use my phone to call the police. I can listen. I cannot judge Gonzalo.

Ana: Well, do I have your permission to accuse Gonzalo of incredible, insane stupidity?

Dr. Suárez: You can tell him how you feel. And he can tell you the same. I'm not sure that leveling accusations will be helpful.

Ana (*mockingly*): Really. What would be?

Dr. Suárez: Well, I'm here to explore your options once I know more about your situation. That's my job.

Ana: Your job. Describe it. In a nutshell.

Ana (*reading titles of books in office*): *Understanding Human Behavior, Love and Family Conflict: Theories and Resolutions, The Analysis and Diagnosis of Violence.* These sorts of things, *doctora?* Are these the kinds of things you deal in?

Dr. Suárez: The books, well, they're someone else's ideas. They've helped me learn about these "things," as you call them. But nothing's a hundred percent.

Ana: Oh, yes, some things are, *doctora.* Tati's dead. That's a hundred percent.

Dr. Súarez: Yes, Tati is dead. That's a fact you can't change. But you and Gonzalo facing what happened in the woods. Maybe that's something you can.

Ana: But I don't know how.

Gonzalo: Ana likes guilt better than me. Dr. Suárez. Why do you think she ran away and has kept running all around Texas and now to California? But I'm going to settle it for her, so she can make her bus on time, okay? I'm guilty. Now is everybody satisfied?

Dr. Suárez: Not me. There's a lot I don't yet understand. Let's just talk. What do you say? I won't be a referee in a fight, but I can hear you and Ana out. How about it?

Ana: I'm going to say what I want. Tati's not coming back. You said it yourself. I must speak for him.

Gonzalo: You're not the only one who can talk for Tati. He's my son too. No matter what hell I perpetrated on him.

Ana (*hesitantly*): Maybe you're right, *doctora*. But can we talk separately?

Gonzalo: It's all right, *doctora*. She's entitled—I guess.

Dr. Suárez: Which one wants to go first.

Gonzalo: She's leaving on Sunday.

Dr. Suárez: Well, Ana?

Gonzalo (*to Ana*): I'll see you outside.

Ana: You go on. I can get a ride to *Tía's*.

Gonzalo: Whatever you want. Whatever you want.

Blackout

SCENE V

Dr. Suárez: Where shall we begin?

Ana: This is hard, *doctorcita*.

Dr. Suárez: We'll take our time. Just start anywhere you can.

Ana: Well, now that I have the chance to talk to a totally impartial person, I suddenly don't want to say how I feel about Tati, Gonzalo, and me.

Dr. Suárez: Well, if you can't talk about Tati, Gonzalo, or you, what can you talk about?

Ana: Ask me something.

Dr. Suárez: Why can't you live here anymore?

Ana: Because it's of no use. Just a bunch of goat ropers is all I have for a family. Not much else. My Tati, well, they wanted to turn him into one as well. I was going to leave Gonzalo right around the time, the time Tati—well, I'm not going to talk about any of that.

Dr. Suárez: It's okay. What's taking you to California?

Ana: I hear there's a lot of real good stuff going on out there. It's like a real big house of love, *una casa de amor—grandisimo*. Everybody together. That's what I aim to find living out there.

Dr. Suárez: What do you mean?

Ana: Love, *doctora*. L-o-v-e.

Dr. Suárez: You can't find it here?

Ana: Nope. You ever hear of this place being anything more than pickup trucks filled with mud, hay, and—*con perdón*—shit. With guns in trucks, in the living room, in the kitchen, under the bed. Here, there's just a "get rid of it" way of life. You know, if it runs, shoot it. If it smells different from you, spray it with disinfectant, except for the dirty pickup truck.

Dr. Suárez: California. San Francisco. I marched around a lot, demonstrating against the war. I know a little about what you're feeling. I finished school two years ago out there. But I wanted to test out my ideas here, back home.

Ana: Are you staying here forever?

Dr. Suárez: I can't say.

Ana: Yeah, well, you've been places outside of Texas. You have an education. You have some choices about working, living. Not me. When I took off for these last twelve months, I did some thinking of my own. For the first time. And I found out that I couldn't take the place. The whole state stinks—up and down and across. From here to the Valley and the Valley across to El Paso and the other way across to Texarkana. People are mean, especially when you're waiting on them, cleaning up after them, or bringing them their chicken fried steaks, French fries, and mashed potatoes with gravy, and garlic toast.

Dr. Suárez: Are you angry at everybody? Even the Mexicanos? Did they order you around?

Ana: Well, sure, especially the rich ones. Especially the men. They wanted to show me who was a *mujer* and who was a *'chuca*. The poor ones, well, we worked alongside each other, and we had our fights. Some of the men working the grounds smacked their lips when they saw me. "*Ven aquí y siéntate en mis regazos.*" I told them to cut out the crap.

Dr. Suárez: What'd they answer?

Ana: They laughed. That's what they did. They laughed, long and hard. But now and then a few would shut up or get all embarrassed.

Dr. Suárez: That must have been hard for you. You didn't have any other defense, did you? I imagine it will be a long time before a lot more men start crying with us instead of yelling for favors from us.

Ana: Everything they did seemed to put me down. I use to think that if I left the goat ropers behind, I'd be a free woman for once, earning my own money. No hassles. No husband lording me around. My Tati. I didn't want him to grow up this way. In a place where every year claims or maims men on some hunting trip or farm accident.

Dr. Suárez: Tell me a little more.

Ana: Don't you understand what I mean? Why, every step we take white men rule. Even in our "time off," we go for country western over *conjunto*. We even speak with these awful drawls. We sometimes forget who we are up here in redneck country. A lot of us seem to like it, too. We giggle or get embarrassed with our Spanish. We act as if we are supposed to be white and that we accidentally got tainted brown through some awful mistake God made.

Dr. Suárez: Is that how you see yourself? As someone who has been raised to—

Ana: Stay down on the farm. Yep. I mean yes. Well, I guess saying "yep" is more in keeping with what I'm supposed to be.

Dr. Suárez: You're trying to put words in my mouth, Ana.

Ana: Uh, sorry.

Dr. Suárez: I started to say that you feel that you don't have any choice but to imitate white people, right? People who rule the roost, right?

Ana: Uh, maybe.

Dr. Suárez: I don't believe that anybody—white or brown—can probably tell you how to live, Ana.

Ana: Are you saying that I'm wrong?

Dr. Suárez: What do you believe about yourself? That's important. Whether or not you stay or leave.

Ana: Oh, I'm leaving. No question.

Dr. Suárez: Whether or not you figure out a few things with Gonzalo?

Ana: Gonzalo isn't part of this. He took Tati with him, knowing that I had specifically asked him to leave him at home with me, asleep like any five-year-old should be. We had talked about it plenty before, and he'd agreed with me. I don't care about his tears afterwards, his guilt, or his blaming himself. Tati didn't have to die, *doctora*. The only good thing about his dying is that he won't ever have to accept this tough guy routine.

Dr. Suárez: I use to ask the same questions. Why did we see ourselves through the eyes of the Anglos? It didn't make sense, and it made me angry. As a *doctora*, it angers me in a different way. I try to use my *rabia* in another way. It works. Sometimes.

Ana: Couldn't for me. I can't restrain my feelings.

Dr. Suárez: Well, to be honest, I still want to scream sometimes.

Ana: Yeah? I can think of at least five things right away to scream about. But I'll save it for later. You think if maybe I'd yell every day, I could deal with my life?

Dr. Suárez: I'm not up on scream therapy. Children I know seem to get a lot out of it. But their *padres* don't much go for it.

Ana: Scream. Maybe that's what I should have done at Gonzalo instead of leaving the way I did? Maybe. I don't know. I sort of liked going around the state and dealing with all those jerks.

Dr. Suárez: Is everyone else but you a jerk?

Ana: Are you trying to pull *doctora* rank on me?

Dr. Suárez: I was just asking a *mujer*—a true and blue *mujer* question. From one *'chuca* to another.

Ana: You—a *'chuquita? Pero cómo? A ver, cómo?*

Dr. Suárez: Yeah, once upon a long time ago. But it wasn't like today in the big cities. We were strictly backwater—no real tough gangs. But we had a style.

Ana: Want to talk about it?

Dr. Suárez: No.

Ana: Ah, I think I know something *la doctora* is sensitive about, right?

Dr. Suárez: No.

Ana: Well, can we take turns talking about what we are sensitive about?

Dr. Suárez: Sure. Flip a coin.

Ana: No, that's okay. I'll go first. Anyway, I'm leaving Sunday, remember. So, I better get in my two bits.

Dr. Suárez: Yeah, and there's no charge for talk between friends.

Ana: Hey, that's right.

Dr. Suárez: So, go on. What do you want to talk about?

Ana: Anything I want?

Dr. Suárez: Sure. It's just between us.

Ana (*making air quotes*): Maybe about the good old days of being a Chicana kid here? Maybe life before marriage? Maybe why I got married? Maybe why I had Tati? Maybe why I wanted to leave Gonzalo?

Dr. Suárez: It's up to you.

Ana: Well, lemme see. Being a Chicana kid, that is, in Central Texas, I think I want to save that for when I'm fifty. And the same for life before marriage. Why I got married, had Tati, well, that's also out of bounds, right?

Dr. Suárez: You decide.

Ana: Well, when you put it like that.

Dr. Suárez: Whatever you want, okay.

Ana: Tía was the one who took me to the dance where I met Gonzalo. We were both fifteen years old. He twirled me around and around to the latest polkas and rock *canciones* and country western all that night. A few months later we got married. Tati arrived when I was eighteen.

Dr. Suárez: Short and sweet?

Ana: Definitely not sweet, except for Tati. I went back to high school after he was born. And graduated. And took a secretarial job in Waco. I'd carpool to work with some *bolillas* and listen to the latest music coming out of California and England. At home, it was this country western junk all the time, except for when Gonzalo turned on the daily Mexican hour on the AM station.

Dr. Suárez: Yeah, the sweetest time of the radio day. I listened to the Chicano hits, the *canciones* from Mexico. Everything they played I could dance to. Loved, loved, loved the *cumbias*.

Ana: Yeah, all that *música*. Think I'll find it in San Francisco?

Dr. Suárez: I seriously doubt it. It's more Janis Joplin and Jefferson Airplane country. But it may work for you for a while.

Ana: Sure, everything works for me for a while—Gonzalo, Tati, being on the road. Then I escape. Figure out the next place to be. Why'd I run away from his memory—or try to? He's been with me on the road every day. I'd like to figure out how to live with him gone. But the one thing I can't do now is convince myself it was time for Tati to die. I kissed him goodnight and the next time I saw him he was as cold as winter.

Dr. Suárez: Take your time, okay?

Ana: I don't know what to do, if there's anything to be done after a year of nothing happening. I don't have anyone I can talk to who isn't going to defend all those guys and Gonzalo. Not *tía* Juana, not *tío* Estebio, not anyone. They make the sign of the cross and say it was God's will. Well, I say it wasn't. It wasn't. It wasn't.

Dr. Suárez: Is Tati's death what you need to remember? That part of Tati's life? The end of it? How about the beginning? How about the five years before?

Ana: Five years. What does a kid get to do in five years? That's what I can't take. And not to know if he's happy wherever he is. Do you think he's happy—somewhere? I buried him with his favorite toy and blanket. In his favorite play clothes. I pretended I was sending him to some heavenly playground to run and laugh for eternity even if I never saw him again. And from the way I'm living, I probably won't. I want to make sure that some men don't get away with blowing a child away. I want this goat roping town to put down its guns.

Dr. Suárez: Well, the last thing, that's probably not going to happen. But some things, you can deal with a step at a time.

Ana: But does that mean I have to stay here and be reminded every day of what happened?

Dr. Suárez: That's how you've spent the last year—being reminded. I don't think it matters where you're living.

Ana: Where do I start?

Dr. Suárez: Wherever you want.

Ana: Is it entirely up to me?

Dr. Suárez: Absolutely.

Ana: I need to get going. I'll let you know.

Dr. Suárez: Here's my phone number, just in case.

Blackout

Act II

SCENE I

The farmhouse the following morning: Sheriff Phillips is sitting on the living room couch, bragging to Estebio about the deer he and his son have recently bagged.

Sheriff Phillips: It was this big thing, Tebio. Wuy-y! We caught it off guard—didn't even know we were there.

Estebio: Sure. Sure. I want to see the head, with the blood still on it before I believe you. How come you're always bagging 'em but we have never gotten to taste some of that deer meat or seen even one stuffed head in the last ten years?

Sheriff Phillips: Believe me, it's true. Dwayne and me, we got us the best and biggest deer. I'll bring you a couple of pounds of deer sausage next weekend.

Estebio: Hell, man, you owe me at least one hundred pounds.

Sheriff Phillips: You just wait. I'll have Corine get them ready, and I'll be here first thing next Saturday. That is, if your Juana will fix me a Mexican breakfast as a thank-you for my gift. Okay? Now I'm counting on you. By the way, where's that niece of yours? My deputy said she's been calling him since he came on duty late last night. She called me this morning asking me to come over here first thing. So here I am. Yours truly at your service. You figure she still got that kid of hers on her mind?

Estebio: That and getting out to California. She's mixed up real good. Remember how she took off straight from the cemetery last year? We didn't hear a peep until she showed up at our door yesterday. She was talking about how's she's going to settle this thing about Tati once and for all and vamoose to Frisco. Well, her *tía* and me, we're upset 'cause she wants to blame the family—Gonzalo especially—for Tati's death. These things just happen. Leave it to God.

Estebio (*tentatively*): Maybe it was Tati's time to go. That's what we told her back then. Can the law do anything? I mean, no one's responsible, right? It was an accident. Gonzalo didn't mean any harm. He was just doing what a lot of daddies do, taking his boy with him, showing him the ropes.

Sheriff Phillips: Well, I ain't touching one *hombre* just 'cause she says so. I mean, everybody, including the D.A., said it was an accident. It's a shame. I'm not saying that I don't feel for Ana and Tati—and you all. I know if it was my grandchild I would have felt like taking care of whoever did it myself. I like to hunt a deer same as anybody, but a child's a child.

Estebio: You saying we don't care about our kids?

Sheriff Phillips: Sure. Sure, you do. Just seems like accidents happen all the time among ya'll's people.

Estebio: Oh, hell, Phillips. Cut it out. You're a lying—

(*The front door suddenly opens and Ana strides over to the two men.*)

Ana: Sheriff Phillips, you ready to talk? I need to figure out my next move before I leave town.

Sheriff Phillips: Yep. You bet. What time you going?

Ana: Six o'clock bus. I should be in Frisco in about three days.

Sheriff Phillips: Yeah, and damn tired, I imagine.

Ana: Not as tired as I am of all this business. All this lying and denying and refusing to answer a few simple questions about my son's accidental death. No, his murder, I meant to say his murder.

Sheriff Phillips: Watch what you say, girl.

Ana: You know something I don't, sheriff? Got some deal going with the

D.A.? You, Gonzalo, and the guys work out an arrangement you can live with until someone ends up snitching?

Sheriff Phillips: Hold it right there, Miss. Just calm down and get on with your business. Hurry up now. Got me other things to do on this fine day.

Ana: Not before you give me some answers about Tati. Tío, I'd like to talk to Sheriff Phillips alone. *Por favor.*

Estebio: Oh, okay.

Estebio (*to Sheriff Phillips*): I want to see some of that sausage.

Sheriff Phillips: Girl, I got no answers to anything—from who pulled the trigger to whose slug made the fatal shot. You left town in a huff. So there's nothing to talk about. I'm just here because I'm a good public servant answering a call.

Ana: You can answer this call by telling me the truth. The right answer to all the notarized letters I've sent you over the last year.

Sheriff Phillips: Well, I don't think anybody has the answer for you. The only questions to ask so far as I can see is, number one, what was a child doing with a bunch of grown men with rifles hunting deer, and, number two, how negligent were they in not knowing his whereabouts? These are the questions in my mind. And what letters you talking about anyway? My deputy handles all the mail. And I haven't seen anything from you cross my desk, notarized or otherwise.

Ana: Don't worry, I have copies of the letters for you. About your questions. They're my exact questions too. Who'd you ask? What'd they say? What'd you find out?

Sheriff Phillips: Not a single thing. *Nada.* Like you folks say, *nada.* So, case closed.

Ana: But you're not the final word on this. How about the D.A.? How about the coroner? Where have they been all this time?

Sheriff Phillips: Busy, woman, busy with real murder and thieving cases.

Ana: Listen, sheriff, I'm asking you to deal with a group of men who were with my son when he was shot. Someone shot him dead.

Sheriff Phillips: What you asking me to do?

Ana: Reopen the case. It's that simple. Reopen the case of Sebastian Marcos.

Sheriff Phillips: I'll have to see the D.A.

Ana: You do that.

Sheriff Phillips: Meanwhile you're just leaving without finding out what he says? You might come back in another year and find out nothing's been done.

Ana: Don't worry about my whereabouts, Sheriff Phillips. I know where I'll be. And your people will know where to find me.

Sheriff Phillips: Real sure of yourself, aren't you?

Ana: Like never. They got some good lawyers these days willing to take on civil rights cases, you know.

Sheriff Phillips: Oh, now, you ain't thinking Tati's one of *them*, are you?

Ana: Just like I said, sheriff, there's no need for you to worry about what I'm doing. You just do your job.

Sheriff Phillips: Trying to panic me into action, are you?

Ana: You must not have heard me, sheriff. I know what I'm doing. Your only problem is to remember that you're supposed to help two of your con-sti-tu-ents, Tati and me. (*Waves her packet of letters at Phillips.*)

Sheriff Phillips (*a bit stunned and taken aback*): Woman, you took off. What you complaining about my doing or not doing anything at all? And what's that you're sticking in my face?

Ana: Sheriff, you're either a bit mixed up or deaf. Whether I left or stayed didn't matter as far as the law is concerned. You're supposed to do your job—unless, of course, part of your job is to ignore the death of a child who is Mexican and who dies in the presence of Mexicans and who you think died because "those people" just don't care.

Sheriff Phillips: But don't you think it'll look bad for your folks? Be a bit like laying some more salt on the wound Tati's death has caused. Go easy on Estebio, on Juana, they brought you up. Gonzalo, he's your husband, woman.

Ana: Sheriff Phillips, 370 days ago, a very beautiful *niño* was killed "accidentally." But we live by the law, don't we? And that requires that we find out the circumstances of such a death, doesn't it?

Sheriff Phillips: Okay, look here. I'm listening if you hurry up and tell me ex-act-ly what you want me to do.

Ana: I want you to do whatever is necessary when a child dies under questionable circumstances. Plus, I want you to show me the records of what's been done about Tati's death. I want you to show me what the D.A. has done. I want you to do your job. That's what I want you to do.

Sheriff Phillips: It's going to be tough. Why don't you leave it alone? Go on out west. Leave your family in peace.

Ana: Like I said, Sheriff Phillips, I want you to do your job. My lawyer will be touch with you.

Sheriff Phillips: Your lawyer? When'd you go and hire yourself a lawyer?

Ana: She'll be in touch, and she'll ask you the same questions I asked you, only she will put them in writing. I don't plan to let you forget that my child should be alive and giving his mother and father holy hell this very minute.

Blackout

SCENE II

The evening of the following day. Ana is standing near Tati's grave. Her suitcase and bird cage are lying to the side. She is dressed in a long flowing dress and sandals. Dr. Suárez is with her.

Ana: Thanks for driving me out here. Keeps me from having to take my chances and hitching a ride to get the bus out of this place. (*She fingers some flowers she brought to place on Tati's grave.*)

Dr. Suárez: Happy to do it. (*She bends over to read the headstone.*) Tati, *cielito lindo de mi mundo.* Who decided on this?

Ana: I did. I sent instructions from Texarkana.

Dr. Suárez: You made a wonderful choice.

Ana: I wanted to put his baby picture and the date of his birth on the headstone. But it costs. The more you want on it, the more money they want. So I opted to tell him what he means to me on sunny, cloudy, or rainy days. Tati was *el cielito lindo de mi mundo.*

Dr. Suárez: That's a beautiful way to remember your son.

Ana: Well, Tati kept me firmly on the ground. I was trying to raise him up with love. Sometimes, when he would get restless or cry, I'd take him outside, especially at dusk or night, and together we'd play a game of sky watching.

Dr. Suárez: Tell me about it.

Ana: Well, we, we— Sorry, he's the only one I can play it with. (*She looks at Tati's grave.*) Oye, m'ijo, Mami has to leave for a while. There's no use pretending that you're just taking a nap and will be up any minute.

Dr. Suárez: If you want, I can go over there and leave you here so you can be alone. (*Glances at her watch.*) Your bus has already left. There won't be another one until about midnight.

(*Ana takes Amorcito out of his cage.*)

Ana (*addressing Amorcito*): You and I are behind in getting to Califas and all the love fests going on out there. Whaddaya think that means? (*Pretends Amorcito responds.*) I think you don't know what the hell you're doing. You're dragging me all over the world while you figure out if you hate Tati's death more than you love Tati's life. (*Reverts to herself.*) Now don't get smart with me, *pajarito*. You're talking in riddles now, and that's all I get from everybody else. So stop it.

Dr. Suárez: What do you think Amorcito means?

Ana: I dunno.

Dr. Suárez: When I have private conversations with myself, it's usually because I already have my answer. Do you love Tati more than you hate his death? For starters, yes or no is a good enough answer.

Ana: Yes. Yes. Yes.

Dr. Suárez: Okay. Good enough. Now then, how much do you hate his death?

Ana: As much as I could hate anything. Is that plenty enough?

Dr. Suárez: I'd say so. One of those pesky four-letter words.

Ana: Like l-o-v-e. Another pesky word. Hate, love. Love, hate.

Dr. Suárez: You'd think it would be obvious which is best.

Ana: Yeah, you'd bet your life on it and choose l-o-v-e like Martin Luther King.

(*From behind them a voice can be heard, then other voices.*)

Gonzalo: But he also knew just exactly how to make them squirm.

Blackout

SCENE III

Gonzalo stands near Tati's grave. Juana and Estebio are with him. Juana and Estebio are dressed up, and she carries some flowers.

Ana: What are you doing here?

Juana: We're paying our usual visit like we do once a month.

Ana: Oh, sure, this late in the day. Come on, I'm no fool. You're spying on me.

Estebio: We come out here once a month to clean Tati's grave.

Juana: Gonzalo said you might come here before you left. We wanted to talk to you, ask you to stay, ask you to live with us again. (*Hands Ana the flowers.*) These are for you.

Ana: Stay with you?

Juana: *M'ija linda,* you're part of *la familia.* You can have your old room back for as long as you want.

Ana: I'm leaving.

Estebio: We just want to help. We don't care about the past.

Ana: I'm leaving.

Gonzalo: Martin Luther King. You were talking about him. The little I've read about him in the papers, he seemed to be all right. A good man. Had his principles. Like Chávez. Yeah, that one. The farm workers' leader. César. César Chávez. You going to work with him when you get to California? Or you joining a commune in Frisco? Which *casa de amor* you planning on staying in, *linda*?

Ana: I doubt Chávez would take me in. He likes people with more principles than I have, who have what the good *doctora* would call love. I think I'll leave Chávez alone. What do you think, Dr. Suárez?

Dr. Suárez (*ignoring Ana; greeting Juana and Estebio and addressing them*): Why are you ready to welcome her back?

Gonzalo: Guilt, *doctora.* Simple guilt. Ask Estebio why he goes to confession all the time. Ask me why I don't even know my name some days and sleep for hours on others. Yeah, ask all of us about our guilt. We were all planning on a good life until we blasted Tati away with some discount store shells stuck in some secondhand shotguns. We couldn't bring down one deer. Instead we shot to death a child who wasn't even the right size and shape of our prey.

Juana: Gonzalo, we're not guilty of anything. *Nomás Diosito podrá decir. ¿Verdad?* Your *tío* and I feel it's time to bring the family back together, and that includes you as well as Ana. *Pueden vivir te nuevo con nosotros.* We can make a life together again. *¿Verdad, viejo?* You tell them, Estebio.

Estebio: Your *padres* left you, Ana, in our care when they died. You were six years old. *Y desde ese tiempo* your *tía* and I have watched over you, and Gonzalo and your Tati. *Porque son nuestros. Mira,* Gon, when you married our Ana, we said come live with us. That's what we said, and we meant it. Nothing can change that.

Ana: *¿Puedo responder?*

Gonzalo: Do you just want to argue?

Ana: Is that what it sounded like, *feo?* No, I'm trying to figure out what kind of deal this is that Tía and Tío are laying on you and me in the name of *la santa famila* we're supposed to represent. Gonzalo *de mi vida,* that everything's the same. (*She turns to face Juana and Estebio.*) It damn sure is not! *Mire,* Tía. I know you and Tío took care of me. I'm grateful. *Jamás los olvidaré por su bondad.* When Gon and I married, that started to change things. And when Tati arrived, well, we had our own family. But you wouldn't have known it from the way you and Tío wanted to be in charge.

Juana: *¿Y cómo?* We were doing what we thought was right. You two were just *niños* having a *niño.*

Ana: No, we were not *niños.* We were not *niños.*

Estebio (*angry and trying to intervene, approaching Dr. Suárez*): *Oiga, no puede decirle algo a esta perra* who's attacking her kin.

Dr. Suárez: What do you want Ana to say to her *tía, señor?*

Estebio (*rebuffing her*): *Estos educados, no saben nada.*

Dr. Suárez: *Señor,* I can neither scold Ana nor give you a sweet and short answer.

Estebio: *Entonces, yo lo haré.* (*Turning to Ana.*) Shut up! Just shut up!

Dr. Suárez (*calmly and forcefully*): It's impossible to go back to the old days with Ana and Gonzalo. *Señor, esos días ya no existen.*

Juana: *Doctora, no regañe a mi marido. Usted no tiene negocios con nosotros.*

Ana: She's here at my invitation.

Dr. Suárez (*to Estebio*): You asked me what to do about Ana. There's nothing I can do about Ana or about you or Juana or Gonzalo, but I can ask some questions.

Dr. Suárez (*turning to each one in turn*): Ana, If you're going to leave, why? Gonzalo, if you're going to see Tati's death as an unresolved scar on your mind, why? Juana and Estebio, if you're going to keep Tati's death a sacred right of God, why?

Blackout

SCENE IV

The family farmhouse living room. It is the morning of the following day. Estebio enters, carrying a toolbox. He takes down the gun and starts to dismantle the gun rack. The noise arouses Juana's attention and she rushes into the room.

Juana: *¿Qué diablos estás haciendo? ¿Qué se metió?* Oh, the gun rack? *Viejo,* are you sure? It was the first thing you put up when we moved here forty years ago.

Estebio: Yep.

Juana: Just married and blessed by the *cura* to have many children.

Estebio: Then why didn't we, *vieja*? Why did Diosito take them away before we got a chance to see them?

Juana: *No fue la culpa de Dios,* Estebio.

Estebio: *Una maldición, vieja.* That's what it was. You kept losing them all. We got lucky when Ana came to us after Diosito took away her *padres.*

Juana: Estebio, I won't listen to anymore.

(Estebio continues to work on the gun rack. He finally reaches up and tears it off its anchors. The wall on which it has been hung suddenly appears, darker in contrast to the surrounding faded walls. He and Juana stare silently at it.)

Estebio: Is it really the first thing I put up, *vieja*? The first thing? I didn't put up the *fotos de mamá y papá*?

Juana: No, that wasn't until later. We were going through the *castaña* one day and found them in their original wrappings—turned face facedown. We took them out and hung them in our bedroom right above the chest of drawers your *mamá* gave us for our wedding.

Estebio: Well, we'll move them in here now. The *jefita* always hated guns. Now she's going to get her way with her fifty-six-year-old son.

Juana: If you say so, *viejo*.

Estebio: Well, what do you say, Juana? Or would you prefer to put the Kennedy over here and Mamá and Papá over there. We got to cover this scar on the wall here. It doesn't look right.

Juana: Look, I don't care. It won't bring Tati back. And it will give us more trouble with Ana for taking so long to change this around. (*Pausing, deliberating.*) I think the Kennedy would look good here, where the gun rack was. And your *mamá* and *papá* should stay in our bedroom, watching over us.

Estebio: Remember all the photos *de* Tati that Ana took? It would be nice to put one on the other wall to replace the Kennedy.

(*Ana enters with a coffee cup in her hands; she is dressed in jeans and a simple blouse. Her hair is arranged in one simple braid. She has overhead Estebio's last remark.*)

Ana: The beautiful sepia of him—the baby picture—would be nice. I'll lend it to you for the rest of your lives, Tía, Tío. Then it'll come back to me. But I don't want any shrines, Tía. No *velas* surrounding him, and no rosaries strangling him.

Estebio: *¿Qué cambió? ¿Qué te pasó?*

Ana: I had a good night's sleep, I suppose. (*She yawns.*)

Juana: Then why are you yawning?

Estebio (*addressing Ana*): *Me parece que no durmiste. ¿Verdad?*
  (*Ana continues to yawn.*)

Juana: I use to braid your hair. *Así mismo.*
  (Someone pounds on the door as Estebio exits.)

Juana (*answering the door*): Gon, *¿cómo te amaneció?*

Gonzalo: *Cansado, pero bien.*

Juana: This woman didn't sleep either.

Gonzalo: Well, maybe I slept a couple of hours. Didn't get any at all, *linda?*

Juana: Just look at her. She's yawning, and I know she doesn't need any more coffee. (*Trying to take the coffee cup while Ana gently pulls it away.*)

Ana: Gonzalo, you should be working.

Gonzalo: You should be halfway to California.

Ana: A bus comes through every day.

Juana: Are we getting to you, Ana? Moving back in with us.

Ana: I'm going to take care of things, Tía. That's what I'm going to do.

Gonzalo: And us, what about us?

Ana: Well, yes, we need to take care of that too.

Gonzalo: What does that mean? Take care of things?

Ana: Tía, can Gonzalo and I have a *momentito* alone?

Juana: *Pues, como no.* (*She exits.*)

Gonzalo: You're staying. That makes sense.

Ana: *¿Y porque?*

Gonzalo: Because we can be together, figure out what to do about Tati.

Ana: It may bring you a lot of trouble.

Gonzalo: But we'd be doing something for our son.

Ana: Yes, we'll be helping Tati together. But that's the extent of it. I won't be staying with you, and I'm still planning to leave.

Gonzalo: You selfish— You selfish— When Tati died, you left, just thinking about yourself. Now you're back here, mixing us all up, and you're still thinking only about yourself.

Ana: Look, Gonzalo, I don't care what you think about me, so long as you're with me on Tati. Let's figure out what happened that day in the woods.

Gonzalo (*nodding slightly*): Yes.

(*Ana takes her luggage from a closet and takes Amorocito out of the birdcage, perching him on her shoulder.*)

Gonzalo: Where will you be?

Ana: I have an appointment with Dr. Suárez.

Gonzalo: You two getting to be buddy-buddy?

Ana: She's a *doctora* and a friend. I need both.

Gonzalo: But if you want someone to listen, I'm here. Juana and Estebio are here.

Ana: Sure. *Oye, cuídate.*

Gonzalo: You too.

Juana (*yelling from the kitchen*): ¡Vengan a desayunar, hijos! Les hice huevos y chorizo.

Ana: You go on, Gonzalo. Tell Tía I'll call her next week.

Gonzalo (*with much emotion*): Que te vaya bien.

Ana (*nodding but talking to Amorcito*): La doctora awaits our arrival. You know any Little Joe tunes? (*She attempts to whistle "Las Nubes."*)

Curtain

Violin Playing

A Play of the Imagination in Two Acts

Characters

Don Eugenio Leopoldo ('Buelo), seventy-year-old, blind violinist; he
    is short and slender, dressed in khakis and a work shirt, and wears
    soft, woven slip-on shoes.
Jonas, an accordionist, dancer, and singer
Irene, a dancer and singer
Estrella, at twelve years old; dressed in a bright blue dress and
    wearing sandals throughout the play
Estrella, at twenty-five, a poet

Time: The past and the present, at times intertwined
Settings: Empty stage, 'Buelo's room, stairs, and a café, at times
    intertwined

Act I

*A sign in a café window announces: "Free Poetry Reading Tonight. All Stories
and Pseudo-stories Allowed. Only Critics Must Pay for Admittance." A young
woman stands somewhat tentatively on one side of the stage. She is slender
and wears jeans, a sweater, and sneakers. She carries a backpack bulging with
notebooks and writing tools. A single long-stemmed wildflower dangles from
a side of the backpack. Placing the backpack on the floor, she acts surprised to
see the flower.*

Estrella (at 25): I lifted it because there it was, hanging from a bush
    on my side of the street and leaning toward me as if it were beg-
    ging to go my way. So I freed it to join me. (*Moving to the center of the
    stage.*) You don't believe me? Well, then you never met Doña Chona.

When I was growing up, Doña Chona lived up the street from us. She heaped herbal cures and recipes upon Mamá. She also loved to walk in Mamá's garden. Lifting a bouquet of flowers and cuttings from it was her favorite thing. (*She imitates Doña Chona's placid chatting to her mother as she picks out her favorite flowers.*) Doña Chona said the only true way to possess a flower is simply to whack it off and be done with it. She thought that there was a curse associated with politely asking its owner for permission to have what she considered a gift from the world to anyone. Mainly to her. (*Taking the flower out of the backpack and gently fingering it.*) My mother pretended not to notice Doña Chona's doings, but later she would go on about how Doña Chona had taken the largest of the roses or tulips or the newest stem from the *pensamientos*. Doña Chona's philosophy has stayed with me. (*Motioning toward her single flower.*) Besides, I don't own a vase or a table to display flowers to indulge myself in their scents. I simply enjoy them up close now and then by stealing them, like Doña Chona. (*A decided shift in tone.*) And then there are the lessons I learned from Don Eugenio Leopoldo, my 'buelo. I'm at this "No Critics for Free Poetry Reading" because of him. (*She pauses to savor this last bit.*) And he's partly behind my notion of only keeping a few things—this pack, a few clothes, my notebooks (*looking down fondly at her feet*) and my sneakers. Well, I do have a place to eat and sleep, but besides that there's not much else I care to have. (*Wanting to dismiss any of her doubts.*) Oh, well, what I think doesn't matter. (*Decisively.*) It's my writing. Now that matters. (*Starts to look in her backpack for a poem.*) When I'm not earning my keep, I write poems and read them in a café like this one, usually for free. Yes, we poets are always doing it for free. Such saints. Well, I'm not a crazy woman, running down the street with my backpack flying behind me and yelling to everyone to pay into a pension fund for the poets of the world. But it would be nice to offer us more than wine, bread, and cheese. Especially when we get squeezed in between the deadly introduction by the master of ceremonies and the real program for the evening. (*Finds a poem, then decides she likes another one better and reads it to the audience.*)

"For Maximino Palomo"
The official history that
traces in pictures and words,

endlessly depicts
in minute detail
the stealing of your honor
the selling of your manly labor,
the pain you endured
as sons and daughters
drifted from you,
met their death
in the hour of thorns and swords
will fail you
just as will history texts
written with the cutting pen of
palefaced/brownstone men who recall 1848
and
forget to tell about
the man who cradled children to sleep,
smoothed their damp hair,
told them stories,
played *la golondrina* on his violin,
and laughed
aloud at dusk

(*She is silent for a moment.*)

Estrella (at 25): That was my *'buelo*, Don Eugenio Leopoldo, playing his violin and laughing and telling stories—usually embellished. I believed pretty much everything in them. And they did push me to dispense with dreams for a big car, the beachfront home. But I keep (*dances around*) a handy Walkman as a musical inspiration for my calling as a shaper of words. (*Laughing at herself and looking down at the lines of the poem in her hands.*) I was afraid I would become more and more, day by day, one of the daughters who drifted away from the love of beauty, which was the gift 'Buelo gave me. Even though we Mexicanos lost the war in 1848 and our rights to keep our language and our heritage, I don't squeeze bitterness into my poems. Every time I open my notebooks a light naturally appears on them. Once I wrote that on an application for a job I did not get. I'm pretty sure saying that thing about the light on my notebooks did me in with the office of personnel. And this was for a job as an artist-in-residence who works with children on creativity. And other such light-filled tasks. Too intense, they wrote in the margin, and they thanked me for coming in. (*Putting the poems back in her pack.*) See there, 'Buelo lost me a job. Well, several jobs. By the time I was born, 'Buelo didn't have what you would call a bringing-home-the-bacon job. He was fifty-eight years old and blind. But he had the job he always held when he wasn't working someone else's land and cattle. He was an actor, storyteller, violinist, and extemporaneous speaker at weddings or funerals. And he did them all for free.

Blackout

(*In the background, Jonas and Irene can be heard singing.*)

> México lindo y querido
> si muero lejos de ti
> que digan que estoy dormido
> y que me traigan aquí.

Don Leopoldo is in his room. An old army cot, two straight back chairs, and a table by the cot make up the room's furnishings. A beat-up metal valise is underneath the cot. A violin and radio are on the table beside his cot. He is tuning the radio and humming México lindo y querido, si muero. . . .

Estrella (at 25) (*standing to a side of the room*): Sometimes around dusk I think a lot about you, 'Buelo. That was the time of the day when we could listen to the radio stations from Mexico. (*Taking his hands in hers and kneeling in front of him.*) 'Buelo, I left here. Not a sin, I know. But I want to always remember those truths you taught me. The ones that showed me who we were by playing music together. (*She stands up, walks around the room, and comes to the center, where she pulls the string for the single light bulb. Don Leopoldo reaches out, searching for his violin case. She hands it to him and helps him take the violin out of the case. He begins to tune it.*)
Estrella (at 25): My 'buelo—Don Eugenio Leopoldo. A beautiful name. One surely made for a storyteller. For a violinist.

(She walks out of the room to sit on a far side of the stage. Twelve-year-old Estrella walks in and sits at the opposite end of the stage.)

Estrella (at 12): I've followed you everywhere, staying at your side, whispering reminders about when you were me. When you dangled your legs over Pola Riley's fence, laughing about her ghost stories. You liked to say that you would grow up to become a storyteller because that would be the best job to have. Remember Pola's Valentine's Day letter you never sent to her?

Estrella (at 25): Yeah, yeah. Not long ago I wrote Pola a Valentine's Day poem. Never sent that one either.

Estrella (at 12): How did it go?

Estrella (at 25): Well, let me see. *(Searching though her backpack.)* Here it is. Want to read it with me?

(They recite it, and Irene and Jonas begin to dance. The light darkens on the Estrellas. Irene and Jonas become the visual focus of attention.)

Both Estrellas:

> Today I remember for the first time
> to write about Pola who took care of me
> and 'Buelo,
> feeding us doses of friendship
> from her jars of sweets.
> Having promised it to myself,
> today
> I looked for a valentine in the 5 and 10 cent store
> for Pola.
> And for myself
> a poem of Pola,
> who took care of 'Buelo and me,
> giving us *lonche*
> and a place to spend the long afternoons,
> a fence to sit on
> and ghost stories to hear
> in between
> bags of pinto beans to clean
> over conversations with

Shirley and Barbara,
her daughters of an Irish father.
A picture in my mind
Pola makes,
rolling cigarettes for Leopoldo's
thrice-a-day habit,
laughing with him into the evening.

That stuff could have killed
him my mother said later,
referring to the home perm tissue paper
Pola used,
not the tobacco itself.

And today I will start my valentine
and send it next year to Pola,
who, for fourteen months, with *Mamá* in the hospital,
kept us securely on our balance wheel
an afternoon at a time.

Estrella (at 25): Why are you always at my side?

Estrella (at 12): To be a guide. To find you when you stray. For Jonas, Irene, 'Buelo, and me to call out to you when you are lost. (*Acting out the next lines.*) To be your guide through the railroad tunnel remembrances. We used white rocks to scribble stories on the tunnel walls. I'm all of us—Jonas, Irene, 'Buelo, and you—watching the soldiers on the train bound for the army base nearby. I'm you pretending to be *la triste*, mimicking her. I'm you, riding your bike to the grocery and getting scared to death halfway there that you're lost forever and will never, ever find your way home again to all of us, to—

Estrella (at 25) (*finishing her sentence*): What made sense, to what 'Buelo reminded me with his three changes of clothes, his violin playing, his stories, his willing to move lightly through the world.

Blackout

(*In his room Don Leopoldo is tuning his violin while listening to the news from a barely audible radio station from Mexico. He leans in closely. Then he starts to play his violin. He stops abruptly and calls out.*)

Don Leopoldo: Estrellita! Estrellita!

(*Twelve-year-old Estrella is sitting on the steps leading to the kitchen of the family home, apparently lost in her daydreams and gazing at the stars. Her grandfather's call startles her.*)

Estrella (at 12): *¿Qué quiere, 'Buelo?*
Don Leopoldo: Come here and bring your clarinet, *m'ija*. I want to hear "The German Waltz" one more time so I can commit it to memory. One more time ought to do it, *m'ijita*.

(*Twelve-year-old Estrella approaches an imaginary screen door and peers in.*)

Estrella (at 12): Okay, but can we play it together, 'Buelo?
Don Leopoldo: Sí, sí. Okay. Okay.

(*Twelve-year-old Estrella turns quickly, dashes up the steps, and enters the kitchen and the house offstage. She rushes out just as quickly, attaching the mouthpiece to the rest of the instrument; the sheet music is tucked under one of her arms. Back in her grandfather's room, she pulls up a chair, sits down, and throws the sheet music open onto the cot. Taking a deep breath, she launches into the piece without warming up. She plays "The German Waltz" once. Don Leopoldo listens closely and hums along.*)

Don Leopoldo: Now we can play it together. (He taps out a rhythm for them to follow, and they play "The German Waltz" slowly and delicately.)

(*Twelve-year-old Estrella rises from her chair and goes over to an imaginary window.*)

Estrella (at 12): The Milky Way is out. The Big Dipper is out. The Little Dipper is out.
Don Leopoldo: Are they full of *chocolate mexicano, m'ijita?*
Estrella (at 12): Oh, yes, 'Buelo, and of *canela* from San Luis Potosí sprinkled through it.
Don Leopoldo: Well, bring me a cupful, Estrella. (*Both laugh heartily.*)
Estrella (at 12): Oh, 'Buelo, you and I know only one song together, and I don't even know my part by heart.

Don Leopoldo: That's all right. Someday you'll carry your own versions of our *música* in your heart just like I carry the songs from the *conjuntos* in mine.

(*Music can be heard in the background, first only to him as he leans in its direction.*)

Don Leopoldo: Do you hear that sound, *m'ija?*
Estrella (at 12): Which one?
Don Leopoldo: The one coming from beyond Doña Chona's house, the one beyond the cooing of the *paloma* and the hooting of the owl.
(*She turns in the direction in which he is leaning.*)
Estrella (at 12): Oh, yes, I can make it out. Are they the ones you played with in Crystal?
Don Leopoldo: Yes, yes. Often several nights in a row. We played and danced down the streets and made the dust rise in joy.

(*They both laugh deeply.*)

Estrella (at 25) (*standing in a corner of the room*): Maybe we could go back there now, 'Buelo, and be with them and make up stories again and set them to songs and dances?

(*The voices of a group singing Mexican love songs blend into the scene. Irene slowly moves across the stage to the beat of the music, seemingly connecting the two Estrellas, who then walk around Don Leopoldo's room. They take turns reciting a poem. Irene and Jonas dance as Don Leopoldo plays his violin to accompany them.*)

> **Estrella (at 25):**
> With words I am making a life.
> **Estrella (at 12):**
> With words I find flowers
> hidden between rocks,
> with words I harvest corn, pluck peaches.
> Remember the signposts of
> all the towns we drove through
> to work the fields.

Estrella (at 25):
With words I pull ideas apart,
stitch them back together
into intricate lace .
in different patterns,
Estrella (at 12):
biding my time
for the proper moment
Estrella (at 25):
to push aside
the wailing wall
we carry around inside us
and tend the roots in the ground.
Both Estrellas:
Growing
whatever branch will spring up
and make
a new vine
Estrella (at 25):
appear
Estrella (at 12):
possible.

Blackout

(*Twelve-year-old Estrella is leading her grandfather by the hand across his room.*)

Don Leopoldo: What is it you were saying about taking ourselves back to Crystal?

Estrella (at 12): Oh, that we could pack in a second, put the Big and Little Dippers and the Milky Way in our hip pockets, and the *canela* from San Luis in our back pockets and be gone—like her. (*Twirls around, looking for twenty-five-year-old Estrella.*)

(*Don Leopoldo rises and faces twelve-year-old Estrella. He places his belongings into his metal valise.*)

Estrella (at 12) (*downhearted*): But I know it's to Tío's you must go. What will I do while you're gone?

Don Leopoldo: Keep playing your clarinet and writing in your notebooks.

Estrella (at 12) (*brightening somewhat*): Things for remembering you by, 'Buelo?

Don Leopoldo: And for remembering the family with words that are soft, words with edges that are deft and sure, words that are curved one into the other, flowing together.

(*Twenty-five-year-old Estrella enters and sits on an edge of the stage. Don Leopoldo takes his valise from twelve-year-old Estrella and walks away, making his way with his homemade cane, calling out to his son as he goes.*)

Don Leopoldo: *Hijo, hijo, aquí vengo.*

Blackout

Act II

Buelo has died while at his son's home. The family has returned from his burial. Twelve-year-old Estrella is sitting on the steps leading to the kitchen, writing in her notebook.

Estrella (at 12): They wouldn't let any accordion music be played for you, 'Buelo. The Father said it would bring dishonor to the church. Gypsy music, he scoffed at *Mamá* when she made her request to him. Pure gypsy music is what that is, and we cannot dishonor the dead either, *señora*. So, my mother, in deference to the Father, let you be buried without anyone playing a note—not one note. Not even a violin. Not even just a little bit of a violin. I wanted to do something very . . . wild.

(*Stands up and sings a capella.*)

> Despierta mi bien, despierta,
> mira que ya amaneció.
> Ya los pajaritos cantan.
> La luna ya se metió.

(*With the last lines, she stands on the top step.*)

Estrella (at 12): *Ya se metió la luna.* Yes, 'Buelo, the moon has gone home for a few hours along with the Milky Way and the Big Dipper and the Little Dipper and the *canela* from San Luis Potosí for our *chocolate a la mexicana.* (*Exits.*)

(*Twenty-five-year-old Estrella walks around an empty stage looking for Don Leopoldo's belongings.*)

Estrella (at 25): I don't know how his violin disappeared. If it was left at Tío's or was dumped somewhere, hidden in a closet, put in the weekly garbage pickup. I never saw it again.

   (*Stopping at different points on stage.*) Somehow the room he lived in was emptied out right away. Just like that, the radio was gone, the cot, his rosary. I would walk into it looking for his stories and the dancers and musicians, the dreamers he conjured up for me and him. I could only hear the silence of his death . . . until I made myself pay attention. (*Completes her tour of the room and lies down in the middle of it.*) I started to dream about Jonas, Irene, 'Buelo, and me in Crystal.

(*Twenty-five-year-old Estrella falls into a dream. Irene and Jonas enter. Irene continues into the audience, carrying a violin case, and sitting down near the front. In the dark, Estrella awakens and exits the stage.*)

Jonas (*playing his accordion and swaying in unison with it*): Mine is a simple wish for you campesinos of Crystal—to bring you the chance to find either the beginning or the ending of a story, the way you imagine that it could begin or end.
Irene (*holds up the violin case*): We would like to discover the true secret of this.
Jonas: What are you seeking?
Irene: The knowledge of the owner of this. (*Again holds up the violin case.*)
Jonas: Ah, a musician, like me!
Irene: No. No.
Jonas: Well, go on and open the violin case and show me what's there.

(*Irene goes up to the stage, unlocks the violin case, and, with Jonas, peers into it. She gingerly removes its contents one by one—a stub of a pencil, a very worn notebook, and a dusty diary. Jonas places each item on a small table.)*

Jonas: How did you come by the violin case and all its possessions?

Irene: My aunt.

Jonas: Were they already in the violin case?

Irene: Yes, just like this. Her mother gave it to her.

Jonas: Just as it was?

Irene: Yes. Yes, just like this.

Jonas: Has no one ever used them?

Irene: Not that I know of.

Jonas: Why not?

Irene: Well, many people thought that it didn't make sense to put these things in a violin case. Others couldn't write. That was their reason. The rest of us were afraid to touch them.

Jonas: Afraid? Of what?

Irene: Afraid of making fools of ourselves by writing things people would laugh at, writing down things we saw, said, heard. (*Pauses.*) Some of them were funny or sad—even truthful. You know, things we might want to pass along. (*Pauses.*) It's very sad that we didn't think we had anything worth passing along.

Jonas: And how did your aunt end up with the case in the first place?

Irene: It was left behind by one of her cousins, left in a house that she and her family lived in after the cousin and his family left to go north for the crops one summer.

Jonas: Why did he leave it there?

Irene: It had been going from one family member to another for a long time, from the time of the revolution in Mexico when a relative—a man—brought it over with him after he fled the country. My aunt said that at one time a violin had been in it, but by the time the relative got to this country he only had the case because he had to trade the violin for food during the war.

Jonas: Why did he put the pencil, notebook, and diary in it?

Irene: My aunt only knew some hearsay about that. She said that the relative hoped for someone in the family to—

Jonas: To what?

Irene: I'm not sure, exactly. But the relative hoped that someone would learn how to love to do what his great-grandfather had loved to do.

Jonas: And what was that?

Irene: To make beautiful stories for us all. My aunt liked to say: *Alguien que tenga el gusto del cuento de la vida dentro si mismo.* Someone who carried within a joy for storytelling.

Jonas: Without the violin?

Irene: We laughed about that. Everyone thought that the long-gone relative was a very truly sad case and that maybe it was crazy to think that anyone might come along and take his advice. They'd look at the violin case, shake their heads, and ask, "A violin case with no violin?" They'd ship it along to another relative with a note to keep it hidden.

Jonas: The point wasn't really to play the violin, then.

Irene: Oh, I don't know for sure. To me it doesn't seem that it was all that important to play the violin. My aunt believed it was meant to show us we could become artists.

Jonas (*taking Irene's hand and leading her across the stage*): I know someone who might just might be. . . . She's traveling with our troupe for a few days.

Irene: Who? Who?

Jonas: The relative's hoped-for artist.

(*As twenty-five-year-old Estrella enters, on the wall opposite her are flashing slides of family and friends, living their daily lives. She passes by them slowly and speaks a poem to the audience. Irene and Jonas dance as she speaks. She caresses the photographs on the walls, with her voice breaking toward the end.*)

Estrella (at 25): I should be trying to start some begonia plants.

There's the dirt my father
put in two grocery sacks
and
drove down 90 miles to me

and there
are the pots my mother
saved
for me.

So:
I should be trying to start some new begonia plants.

I should let them grow into pink or red blossoms
for you
to reach toward you in this way before
you go off into the fields
to organize the tomato pickers, beet pickers,
melon pickers, cucumber pickers, apple pickers . . .

who are out there
all
year
long
bending over,
tending others' crops
not growing begonias
in their backyards.

So:
I should be the crazy year-long gardener
plowing up my window box planter
growing begonias
sending them to you
for your desk piled high with sheets announcing
strikes, boycotts, marches.

You know what you are up to
and
I know what I am up to
for we are people
who have always bent down
to touch blossoms: of our own making

Blackout

Estrella (at 25) (*as she was at the beginning, in the café for the poetry reading*):
I used to worry that if 'Buelo and I never made it back to Crystal, I
would never learn anything good about us. Not enough to use the
dreams he handed to me each day. Not enough to write things down.

(Jonas, Irene, and Don Leopoldo are at different points around the stage in semi-darkness. As Estrella moves through the scene, overhead lighting focuses on her and them at different intervals.)

Estrella (at 25) *(surprising herself)*: But I didn't abandon 'Buelo. I didn't forget our stories.

Jonas: No, you didn't. His violin playing was your way to the poems.

(Jonas and Irene remove the violin case to a side, returning to it the pencil, notebook, and diary. They bring out a small desk and cover it with a lace cloth, put a bouquet of small cuttings and blossoms in a vase on it, add a fresh sheaf of paper to the desktop, and lay some fountain pens close by. They add a chair. An overhead light indicates that sun is pouring through it. In the background, music—a combination of different traditional and contemporary Mexican/ Chicano works can be heard. Jonas and Irene exit.)

Estrella (at 25) *(in the imaginary café)*: As I was saying earlier, I only carry a couple of things with me and don't have any real place to live. Well, actually I sort of have a place, but, well, I try to ignore the fact because Chimino, our secret name for 'Buelo, never had a real place. *(She turns and looks at the desk and light).* I thought I would do something for him by giving up, well— *(She stops and seems amused at her continuing litany of self-denial. The light falls on 'Buelo, who is sitting in a chair. He turns on his radio and starts tuning his violin. Estrella goes to his side and attempts to sit on the floor next to him.)*

Don Leopoldo: Sit in the chair, Estrella. You're too old to sit on the floor.

(Twelve-year-old Estrella enters and sits quietly on the floor.)

Don Leopoldo: Listen *m'ija*, all this we did here in my room—the violin playing. It was all true enough to the heart, to the soul. You're a watcher of the things that go on—inside and outside us. *(Pausing and deliberating.)* Go write them down.

Blackout

(Twenty-five-year-old Estrella is sitting in the same chair but now facing the desk. She begins to write. In the background the faces of farmworkers are flashed on a screen. A slow musical incantation and dance begin, and the younger Estrella dances around the desk. The older Estrella continues to write, occasionally looking up to notice the younger. They alternately speak aloud the lines she is writing.)

> I will not let any of us disappear.
> For us I write stories.
> Etchings
> pasted to paper like
> photographs in family albums,
> wild with love,
> insisting
> that
> we are who we claim to be.

(Twenty-five-year-old Estrella hands the sheet to twelve-year-old Estrella and sits in stillness. The younger Estrella takes the sheet and, caressing it, dances away and offstage.)

Curtain

Act II
Colchas, Colchitas

ca. 1980s

Colchas, Colchitas

Carolina stood in front of *abuela* Felipa's long oblong mirror, the one from Vera Cruz. She admired herself in her brand-new bright yellow dress.

She shouted, "Look at what my grandmother made for me!"

Carolina twirled around the rocking chair in her grandmother's bedroom. She didn't care if anyone heard her making a racket. When she twirled again, she tipped over her *abuela*'s sewing basket.

"Oops!"

When Carolina looked down, she almost lost her breath. The floor was covered with pieces of cloth in orange, blue green, red, and pink. She also spotted the bright yellow of her brand-new dress. The pieces were in all sorts of patterns and shapes. Some resembled flowers; some looked like birds. What was Abuelita doing with all this?

That night Carolina took Abuela a cup of her favorite tea, *manzanilla.*

"*Aquí tiene, mi abuelita,*" Carolina said softly.

When Abuela finished her tea, she set the cup on the table next to her. Carolina cleared her throat. Abuela looked up.

"What is it, *mi corazón?*"

"Abuelita, were there any leftovers from the cloth you used for my dress?"

"*Sí, m'ija.* Why do you ask?"

"Well, I was wondering what would happen to them."

Her grandmother smiled and motioned Carolina to come closer. "They will go to make other beautiful things for our family."

"Like what?" Carolina asked.

"*Colchas, colchitas,*" Abuela said. "You've seen them covering all of our beds."

"*¡De veras!*" exclaimed Carolina.

"*Sí,*" Abuela nodded.

Carolina was quiet for a moment, thinking back on the quilts that

Mami wrapped around her in the winter when she and Papi tucked her in and kissed her goodnight.

"Those are all little pieces of dresses?" she asked.

"Not all of them, *m'ijita*. Some are from old shirts and pants that I've saved. Sometimes they come from bright, shiny, and new cloth like the kind I used for your yellow dress."

"Why don't we buy quilts like everybody else does?"

Abuela was silent for a moment. Then, embracing her granddaughter, she said, "Well, we like our home to be full of family treasures. Our home is packed with beautiful things that belong to your mami and papi. To your brother and sister. And to you, Carolina."

With that, she smoothed back Carolina's hair.

Carolina leaned into the crook of Abuela's arm, feeling warm and snuggly. Then Abuela pulled a giant dark blue star from her basket. It was made of silk.

"Oh!" Carolina exclaimed. "It's so big and pretty." Her dark brown eyes grew almost as big as the dark blue star.

Abuela chuckled delightfully. She said, "It is fifty years old and still has its color."

"It's older than you. Older than you and your brother and sister. Older than your mami and papi," Abuela added.

"It's from a dress I wore when I was young and went dancing on Saturday nights with your *abuelo* Roberto. We weren't married then. I've been saving it to make a special quilt. I want to put it with pink and white pieces of cloth. It will be a special present for your mami."

"Is it a surprise?" Carolina whispered.

"Yes, so it must remain our secret, *m'ijita*."

"Oh, *sí*, Abuelita," agreed Carolina.

Then she looked down at her brand-new bright yellow dress. Maybe someday it would become a favorite quilt for someone she loved.

Abuela said, "This *colcha* will be a story about your mother and me. But maybe it can be about you too."

She leaned back in her rocking chair and closed her eyes. Carolina slipped out of the room. She knew that Abuela was going to dreamland for a while. She wondered what Abuela had meant. How could the quilt be about her, too?

Early the next morning, Carolina knocked on Abuela's door.

"*Adelante*," she heard Abuela say.

Carolina stood quietly as Abuela finished tying her shoes.

"Abuelita," she began.

"*Dígame*," Abuela replied, patting Carolina's cheek.

"May I help make Mami's *colcha*?"

Abuela was silent for a moment and looked into her granddaughter's eyes. "Would you like to do that?"

"Yes, I could help make a baby star from the leftover cloth from my yellow dress and add it to Mami's *colcha*."

Abuela reached into her basket. "Well, let's see what we can do." She was smiling. Carolina knew she was going to let her help with Mami's quilt.

"I have the pieces from your yellow dress all together right here."

Carolina laughed and clapped her hands. Then she twirled around Abuela's rocking chair.

Abuela took a pencil and a small star pattern from her sewing table. "Here *m'ija*, we'll trace it together."

They worked until a bright yellow baby star appeared. Then Abuela cut it out and handed it to her granddaughter.

Carolina held the bright yellow baby star up to the light. She liked the way it glowed.

"Where should we put it on the quilt?" her grandmother asked. She had already started to piece together a quilt square from a white piece of cloth.

"Let's put it at the top of the square," said her granddaughter.

Together, they made sure the edges of the star were laid down very flat. Then Carolina handed Abuela a needle, a thimble, and some thread. She watched her grandmother sew the bright yellow baby star on Mami's *colcha*. It was right next to the big dark blue star.

Then she and Abuela laid the square on the floor. Their eyes danced when they looked at the bright yellow baby star.

When Mami's birthday arrived, Carolina and Abuela were ready with their surprise.

"Oh!" Mami exclaimed, laying down her briefcase. "It's so beautiful!" She started to cry with joy. Just then she noticed the bright yellow baby star next to the big dark blue one.

"My, my," she said, stroking it gently.

Carolina smoothed down the front of her bright yellow dress. She said, "It's from my dress, Mami."

Why, it is," Mami replied. She leaned over and gave Carolina a big snuggly *abrazo*.

Then Mami rushed to her bedroom to spread the quilt across her bed. The bright yellow star looked mighty pretty, shining next to the big dark blue star. Both stars were surrounded by pink and white squares. Abuela had added sunrays to Carolina's star.

That night Carolina's mami gave her an extra kiss goodnight, and so did her papi. "*Mi hija linda*, now you know a little bit more about me and your grandmother," Mami whispered as Carolina drifted off to sleep.

The next morning Carolina asked Abuela to show her more leftovers from family dresses, shirts, and pants. Abuela walked over to her closet and opened it wide. Carolina gasped when she saw the neatly stacked rows of cloth. Some were already pieced together. They were ready to become *colchas, colchitas*.

"Are all these from our family?" she asked.

"I'll tell you about them. Let's start with Tío Chuy," Abuela said, pulling several brown pieces of cloth from one stack. "This was once a coat for the cold days he spent outside, working on our rancho."

From that day, Carolina started to find out more about her aunt Lourdes, the doctor, and her great uncle Luis, the herb gardener. Their suits and coveralls were now quilts on her brother's and sister's beds.

Abuela also told her about her great aunt Olivia, the writer, whose pale green cotton dress became a quilt for Papi's favorite couch. He always covered himself with it when he took naps on Sundays. Sometimes when he awoke, he would recall that he had dreamed about great aunt Olivia's stories. Then he would walk over to a bookshelf and pull down one of her books. He would read it late into the night.

Ever since Carolina learned about her family's quilts, she slept beneath quilts Abuela stitched together.

All cozy under one of her grandmother's quilts, Carolina dreamed about her aunts and uncles and her family's history.

Sometimes she dreamed about the *colchas* that she would also piece together.

As she dreamed, the stars outside her window gazed down upon her smiling face.

The casita shared by the Palomo and Acosta families in McGregor, Texas, ca. late 1930s. Box 3, folder 10, Teresa Palomo Acosta Papers, Nettie Lee Benson Latin American Collection, University of Texas Libraries, Austin.

St. Francis on the Brazos Catholic Church, Waco, Texas, where I was baptized. Photograph by Teresa Palomo Acosta, 2018. Private collection of Teresa Palomo Acosta.

Teresa Palomo Acosta,
First Holy Communion,
McGregor, Texas, ca.,
1950s. Private collection
of Olivia García.

Andres y Sabina Acosta 715 Railroad Drive McGregor, TX 1957

Photograph of Acosta family home, McGregor, Texas, with key to the house's
back door. My family moved to this home at 715 Railroad Drive when I was
about ten. A small one-room casita was in our backyard. It moved with us
from our previous home on the same street. My father added a room to a
shed along the side yard. These spaces housed my paternal grandmother
Felipa Alderete Acosta and my maternal grandfather Maximino Palomo for
many years. Private collection of Carolina Tremaine.

Maximino Palomo, my maternal grandfather, the inspiration for my play *Violin Playing*, walking to his casita in the backyard of the Acosta family home in McGregor, 1965. His casita and the yard appear in the play. Private collection of Teresa Palomo Acosta.

Teresa Acosta, Maximino Palomo, Olivia Acosta, and Diana Anaya (*in front*), second cousin of Teresa and Olivia on their father's side, Acosta family home in McGregor, ca. 1960s. Box 3, folder 6, Teresa Palomo Acosta Papers, Nettie Lee Benson Latin American Collection, University of Texas Libraries, Austin.

Sabina and Andrés Acosta, my parents, McGregor, Texas, December 25, 1967. Private collection of Olivia García.

Teresa Palomo Acosta and family dog Fluffy at the Acosta family home in McGregor. The yard is noted in *Violin Playing* as the site where Doña Chona helped herself to my mother's flowers, ca. mid-1960s. Private collection of Olivia García.

Acosta family at St. Eugene Catholic Church, McGregor, ca. 1960s. *Back*: Jesse, Andrés Jr., and Olivia; *front*: Sabina, Andrés Sr., and Teresa. Box 3, folder 10, Teresa Palomo Acosta Papers, Nettie Lee Benson Latin American Collection, University of Texas Libraries, Austin.

"The all-pink doily," crocheted by Sabina Palomo Acosta, ca. 2000s. My mother's textile creations were her artistic legacy. They made their way into my poetry. Private collection of Teresa Palomo Acosta.

Historians María Cristina García, Teresa Palomo Acosta, and Cynthia Orozco at Las Tejanas Symposium held at the University of Texas at Austin, October 16–18, 2003, following the publication of *Las Tejanas: 300 Years of History*. García, Acosta, and Orozco were educated at the graduate level in the aftermath of the Chicano movement. Private collection of Cynthia Orozco.

Ruthe Winegarten and me at book signing held at Resistencia Bookstore in Austin, Texas, in celebration of our multiple-award-winning *Las Tejanas: 300 Years of History*, ca. 2003. Box 3, folder 12, Teresa Palomo Acosta Papers, Nettie Lee Benson Latin American Collection, University of Texas Libraries, Austin.

Act III
Essays

Tejana History as a Poem:
Sara Estela Ramírez and Me (1990)

Jovita González de Mireles:
An Appreciation (1991)

Women from Separate Corners of
the Room: Forging a Collaborative
Pathway to Tejana History
(ca. 2006)

Escritoras Tejanas: Sirviendo la
Gente / Tejana Writers Serving
the People (2018)

Tejana History as a Poem

Sara Estela Ramírez and Me

Seven years ago, I read "Looking for Zora," an essay by Alice Walker in her collection *In Search of Our Mothers' Gardens: Womanist Prose*. In the work, Walker describes her search for Zora Neale Hurston, the important African American folklorist and novelist. Walker provides a vivid account of her visit to a segregated cemetery in Fort Pierce, Florida, where Hurston is buried. Walker hopes to find Hurston's unmarked grave and place a headstone on it. Walker describes her search for Hurston in the neglected cemetery with its overgrown weeds: "'Zora!' I yell, as loud as I can.... 'Are you out here?' I call again, 'Zora, I'm here. Are you?'" Her search proves to be difficult, emotional, and unsuccessful. She places the headstone at the spot deemed mostly likely to be Hurston's final resting ground and leaves. (Walker, 93, 105)

When I read "Looking for Zora," I felt a shared kinship and loss with Alice Walker because I too wanted to know my Tejana literary *abuelas*. Were they also lying in unmarked graves? Where were their essays, fiction, journalism, and poems? Would I ever find them?

A few years later, I saw a reference to someone named Sara Estela Ramírez in a local newspaper, and to her poem "¡Surge!" The opening lines were:

> ¡Surge! Surge a la vida, a la actividad,
> a la belleza de vivir realmente; pero surge
> radiante y poderosa, bella de cualidades,
> esplendente de virtudes, fuerte de energias.

> Rise up! Rise up to life, to activity
> to the beauty of truly living; but rise up
> radiant and powerful, beautiful with qualities
> splendid with virtues, strong with energies!
> (Ramírez in Tovar, 193–94)

This stanza was my introduction to my literary legacy as a Tejana. For many years, I only knew that Sara Estela Ramírez had lived between 1881 and 1910 and had written the poem called "¡Surge!" I paid her no attention because I became preoccupied with my own writing. Although I thought of her on occasion, I remained ignorant of her. Several more years passed. Then, while reading a book of essays on Mexican American women, I noticed a short piece by the historian Emilio Zamora titled "Sara Estela Ramírez: *Una Rosa Roja En el Movimiento*." Upon reading it, I discovered that Ramírez was considered an important activist, essayist, member of the Partido Liberal Mexicano (PLM), and a poet. (Zamora, 163–68)

After reading the article, I spoke with other Chicana poets about themes in their work that draw upon Tejana issues, resulting in works both timely and timeless. I proposed to my *colegas* our need to seek out the precursors to contemporary Tejana writers because our *abuela cuentistas* are hiding in silence in family archives and in other undiscovered places. They can end their silence only with our help. If we remain indifferent to them, the world will never read their words, nor will we know the contentment of their literary companionship.

Here I propose that the history of Tejanas must be explored through literature; suggest that the poetry Ramírez and I created is grounded in a shared history; and relate how Ramírez's poetic perspectives were shaped by her life along the border prior to the 1910 revolution in Mexico, and how mine were influenced in Central Texas during the Chicano Movement.

My point of view is also grounded in intuition. While I know poets do not necessarily write from an autobiographical stance, I believe some themes Ramírez and I have chosen as poets reflect our personal concerns and experiences as Tejanas.

Ramírez was born in Villa de Progreso, Coahuila, Mexico, and grew up during the thirty-four-year dictatorship of Porfirio Díaz, known as the Porfiriato. She trained as a teacher and crossed the border into the United States when she was seventeen years old. Ramírez settled in Laredo, where she took a teaching position at Seminario de Laredo. (Tovar, 32; Zamora, 165)

I know little else about her or her family. Nor do I know what led her to choose life as a poet, teacher, PLM supporter, essayist, dramatist, and publisher of two literary newspapers: *Aurora* and *La Corregidora*. We have only twenty-one recovered works with which to assess her literary output and to illustrate her commitment to write about our people. Perhaps she made this significant choice entirely on her own. Perhaps a family member influenced her. Perhaps she read about the dire economic and political situations under which Tejanos lived during her era. Perhaps simply living day after day in the Porfiriato shaped her into an idealistic young woman who perceived that poetry and politics are sisters and made them her lifelong companions. (Tovar, 113; Zamora, 165)

Between Ramírez's birth, her arrival in Laredo, and her death three months before the onset of the Mexican Revolution of 1910, our people experienced many conflicts and violence on both sides of the United States–Mexico border. These events were influenced both by the Porfiriato and the hostilities that characterized the Anglo-Tejano relationship.

In the border city of Laredo, Tejanos were concerned with issues that affected them on a binational basis. The Spanish-language newspapers reflected this worldview. *El Demócrata Fronterizo* and *La Crónica*, two newspapers that published Ramírez's work, carried news that reveal the circumstances that dominated Tejano life along the border.

These political matters were central to Ramírez's world. Her involvement included public speaking on behalf of PLM leaders and making her home their headquarters in exile. She also joined forces with PLM supporter Juana Gutiérrez de Mendoza in her newspaper *Vespers: Justicia y Libertad*, whose main contributors were female activists. (Zamora, 164–65)

But how was her consuming interest in political activism expressed in poetry? Inés Hernández Tovar has suggested that Ramírez's poetry covers four themes: philosophy, politics, male-female relationships, and sisterhood, all of them grounded in her "understanding of who she is as a human being, a woman, a Mexican involved in social struggle." In her works, her commitment to the rights of our people and her anguish over the personal difficulties of her Tejana sisters emerge. (Tovar, 220, 230)

The three poems I explore below evoke her devotion to the community and to women. These are "Diamantes Negros" (Black Diamonds), "A Juárez" (To Juárez"), and "¡Huye!" ("Flee!").

"Black Diamonds" was written for Yuly, a young orphaned female friend. The ability to overcome personal pain and forge a creative and active life as espoused in "¡Surge!" is the centerpiece of the work. The four-stanza poem acknowledges and destroys obstacles that Yuly faces. Ramírez begins with a straightforward recounting of the tragedy that has struck Yuly. She writes:

> The soul is empty like the cradle
> of an angel who has flown to eternity . . .
> and you know it!

She continues:

> beloved Yuly, I have searched in my heart
> for something beautiful, one ray of sun
> for your sad and eternally orphaned soul
> . . . nothing! I have found nothing
> there worthy of you.

In the succeeding stanzas, she catalogs the positive attributes of "light," a common symbol of hope, and decries her inability to give it to Yuly:

> I want to speak to you of life, and
> death knots up my throat; I want to speak
> to you of laughter and dreams, and tears
> choke me; I want to speak to you of loves
> and enchantments and oblivion arrests
> my words. . . .
> Yuly, there is what
> you expect, love, hope, trust, and . . .
> in vain, I look in vain . . . for the
> souls that are destroyed by pain, hope
> does not exist."

Elsewhere, Ramírez asserts that she and Yuly know that "pleasure, love, illusion, and hope" may be "prohibited" from them. In the final stanza, however, she insists on the desirability of confronting pain and loss:

But, on the other hand, beloved Yuly, there
is something that no one or nothing can
prohibit us. . . . Do you know what it is?
That the darkness of our souls like diamonds
give out light"

(Ramírez in Tovar, 153)

The poet declares that hope triumphs over disillusion, and that wisdom is born from despair. In these final lines she summons Yuly to reject sadness and to live fully.

Tovar has noted that Ramírez's "ideas were developed in a period of severe national unrest" and that the honesty of her words cannot be "disassociated from her life." Thus, Ramírez understands that writing about a private moment of torment showed her commitment to other Tejanas who were also caught in this "unrest." (Tovar, 43)

Moreover, by juxtaposing human frailty with human strength, the poet challenges our hesitancy to resolve loss. Thus, a moment of personal pain creates the opportunity to make positive choices.

"A Juárez" ("To Juárez") is a political poem with relevant lessons and promoting historical awareness. On the surface, the poem seems an ode to patriotism and to Benito Juárez, who some consider to be the savior of Mexican democracy. Yet the work clearly illustrates that Ramírez is more concerned with the strength of the community than with the efforts of any leader.

She writes:

It is true that the deeds of my homeland,
    which I adore,
As well as her heroes
Number in the thousands.
How many pages of gold
In that history of epic songs!
How many sublime strophes on those pages
Where liberty traced her name.

Ramírez stresses that the struggle for freedom has been written in the blood of "indelible red letters." She also declares that a people's valor transcends borders and leaders. As she traces the history of our people's struggles for liberty, Ramírez recalls the symbolism of Mexico's eagle and the "sweet truth" it evokes:

> How many titans, how many gladiators
> With arms of steel destroying
> The thrones of rude oppressors!
> How many fervent lives sacrificed
> On the fields of struggle.

Her vision of freedom connects the past, present, and future. Ramírez states emphatically that "the work for the good is unfinished." She ends the poem with an admonition:

> You, the indomitable Mexican people,
> Look at the past and think of tomorrow,
> You are yet most distant from your goal.
> (Ramírez in Tovar, 159–61)

On one side of the border Ramírez observes a society where Mexicans suffer under the tyranny of Porfirio Díaz. On the opposite side, she witnesses the routine denial of the rights of Tejanos. The poem reflects her politically astute vision, which was drawn from her direct involvement with the radicals of the PLM, who were concerned with the lives of Mexicans regardless of where they lived.

"¡Huye!" ("Flee!"), the third work, reflects a tormented soul, forsaken by fortune and hope. The poem expresses a longing to live in happiness and peace in the politically and economically unstable world forced upon Tejanos. In "¡Huye!" the poet wages an unsuccessful battle in which "Fortune" disdainfully shouts at her: "Flee! you are a stranger. Flee from here!" (Ramírez in Tovar, 165–67; Tovar, 228)

Initially, the poet begs to enter the place of happiness and beauty over which "Fortune" presides:

> I do promise her I will be quiet,
> I do beseech her. . . . She asks for
>   the invitation
> that will admit me to the gathering;
> and the invitation of happiness

I have forgotten . . . it has never been mine!
   My heart has never had it!
   Anxiously I search
in my purse, for anything
I have left there that might serve
But oh! Fortune repeats "Flee. . . ."
And sadly I leave. . . . my step advances,
knocks at the door of Hope
Judging that with her I can leave my faith;
The doors open, thanks to heaven!
It is my consolation.
   I will stay.
                              (Ramírez in Tovar, 165–67)

But Fortune is only teasing her. She is ultimately turned away as Fortune shouts, "for your eyes tears were made! The poet abandons her search:

Tired . . . sad I return to my room
What darkness! What sadness
awaits me there. . . .
I arrive, go in . . . but, I do not stay!
No! The darkness frightens me
and my soul shouts: "Flee from here!"
                              (Ramírez in Tovar, 159–61)

In "¡Huye!" Ramírez employs metaphor and symbolism to explore the conflicts in a life of political struggle. Although she died before the 1910 Mexican Revolution, and before Tejanos quelled the violence committed against them, Ramírez responded to her history in a strong poetic voice, producing works that relate a woman's personal and public journey. She provides in these three works a foundation for contemporary Tejana writers who continue to chronicle the perils that challenge our people's rights.

As a university student, I was still many years from learning about Ramírez. Yet I believe that her influence on me began to take hold on me even then. After spending a semester floundering as a communications major at the University of Texas at Austin, I enrolled in the newly created Mexican American Studies program. Despite my having grown up in the conservative rural town of McGregor, Texas, a small allowance from my father led me to subscribe to *Look* magazine. Through its eye-opening reporting and extraordinary photography, I learned, as a high school student, about the civil rights movement in the United States. This exposure to news from the front, so to speak, played a pivotal role in my inclination to study my people's history.

Once this tendency matured, my family's stories—transmitted through my maternal grandfather and my mother and father—reverberated in my imagination and memory. I wholeheartedly embraced them. The Chicano Movement particularly echoed in my ears through such terms as "Raza Unida," "Chicanas," "Bronze Power," and "Crystal City." It also resounded for me as a history that needed to be told through poetry.

My poems reflect choices I have made, just as Sara Estela Ramírez did, to write about the hearts and souls of our people. These emotional facts of our lives are not available in archives, and Mexican American history books alone cannot express them for us. However, imaginative literature can bring us a more comprehensive understanding of who we are. As Sara Estela Ramírez said in "Diamantes Negros":

> Yuly querida,
> hay algo que nadie, ni nada
> podrá prohibirnos.
> ¿sabes lo que es? Que las tinieblas de nuestras
> almas como diamantes destellen luz.

> Beloved Yuly,
> there is something that no one or nothing can
> prohibit from us. . . . Do you know what it is?
> That the darkness of our souls like diamonds
> give out light.
>
> (Ramírez in Tovar, 153)

Our deeper story lives in this shining darkness, one upon which literary art casts an everlasting light. I end with two of my poems that connect the history that Sara Estela Ramírez and I share.

Balancing Act for Estela Garcia's Childhood

She
Did not know about the composition
Of highwire
Acts
Then.
Still she knew
How to ride
Her *bicicleta*
Balancing herself on worn-out tires.

Other times
Relied
Solely on railroad ties
For proper
Alignment in our contests of
Treading
Tight
Rope
Skills
And
Other
Important
Things:

All seasons skiing in Tejas
On cardboard sleds down the railroad molehills
We called mountains.

Beneath
Ran the underground escape tunnel/route
To homemade rock-chalked stories about
Butterfly hunts
Never
Revealed in first grade

Show and tell
To Mrs. Allen.

Estela
Moved to another town while we were
Still girls and then
(I thought) (I heard) she died young
Still living near a railroad track line
Perfecting
Her
Highwire act
Working without even the
Veiled threat of a net to
Catch
Her
Mistakes.
She used her outstretched arms as poles
To cross the tightrope
Creating her highwire act with
Doled out memories
Of our contest of skills
And our trying wills
To be the favored *mejicanitas*
Of
The neighbors who today, well, have a
Tendency to say to my mother
Sabes, Anna, that Estela, she never
Learned
Like
Your Jesusa,
To make something of herself.

They linger over her with a sorry anguish
Not befitting Estela's highwire act
Of balancing herself with bits, with pieces
Of herself
As foodstuff
To make her journey

On the only sacred ground
She had to herself:
Jump shots
In her imagination
Put to daily practice.

Apparition (ca. 1896)

In the beginning
It was easy to forget them,
And their hands clawing at my door, begging to be let in.

—*No más arrimados eran*
Because that's what I let them be
In the beginning. They were
Bunches *de arrimados*
Holding me to the past,
Holding me to promises
I could not keep.

But

Now they are real pictures and words
Found in a history book.

Now
They stand in front of their *jacales*
And confront my timid sidelong glance.

In one picture they lie dead. Ropes are looped
Around their necks. Texas Rangers sit on their
Horses over them, refusing to meet anyone's gaze.

Now

Each day
They talk to me on my walks—
Wondering when I will put them in my poems.
They tell me how things were
On their *ranchitos*
And how they lost their land in sales

Of 4,000 acres for 200 dollars
Fair and square under Texas laws.

It is impossible to live
With such holy ghosts
As these.

For I cannot breathe
Or get on with anything else
If I cannot
Keep them permanently beloved.

And so I bend in closer
To their faces
And their words jumping out
From history

To say
To them

Stay with me.

For I'm on my way home
Across your plains and unfenced lands
Moving toward you to find

Peace.

I shall not lose you again.
We will find some permanent place
To live together.

It will be our finest entrada.

Sources

Acosta, Teresa Palomo. "Balancing Act for Estela García's Childhood," in *Saguaro* (University of Arizona Mexican American Studies and Research Center) 4 (1987): 15–17. The poem later appeared in my collection *Nile and Other Poems* (Austin, TX: Red Salmon Press, 1999).

Acosta, Teresa Palomo. "Apparition (ca. 1896)" from unpublished manuscript, 1988–90. The poem later appeared in my collection *Nile and Other Poems* (Austin, TX: Red Salmon Press, 1999).

Ramírez, Sara Estela. "¡Surge!" In Inés Hernández Tovar, "Sara Estela Ramírez: The Early Twentieth Century Texas-Mexican Poet." PhD diss., University of Houston, 1984. According to Tovar, "¡Surge!" was Ramírez's last-known writing before her death. Translations of Ramírez's works in this essay are Tovar's.

Tovar, Inés Hernández. "Sara Estela Ramírez: The Early Twentieth Century Texas-Mexican Poet." PhD diss., University of Houston, 1984.

Walker, Alice. "Looking for Zora." In *In Search of Our Mothers' Gardens: Womanist Prose*. San Diego: Harcourt, Brace, Jovanovich, 1983.

Zamora, Emilio. "Sara Estela Ramírez: Una Rosa *Roja en el* Movimiento." In *Mexican Women in the United States: Struggles Past and Present*. Edited by Magdalena Mora and Adelaida R. Del Castillo. Occasional Paper 2. Los Angeles: University of California, Chicano Studies Research Center Publications, 1980.

Jovita González de Mireles

An Appreciation

It is time to honor Jovita González de Mireles.

My tribute is a small step in acknowledging her finely drawn record of the Tejano *pueblo* through her work in folklore, literature, and history.

The best way I can honor González de Mireles is with words, the weapons with which she armed herself to write about, and thus conserve, our people's long history along the Texas-Mexico border. Through her efforts, she proclaimed the compelling sustenance of our oral and written literature.

When González de Mireles carried out her important work, she was the first Texas-Mexican scholar known to collect our tales, legends, and songs. She took the stories she heard in Spanish and shaped them into forceful English versions, thus becoming one of the first Texas-Mexicans to record our literature in English.

"Tales and Songs of the Texas-Mexicans" appeared in *Man, Bird, and Beast*, published by the Texas Folklore Society in 1930. In the piece, González de Mireles wrote: "In secluded communities untouched as yet by civilization, where the people still live in pastoral simplicity, folk-lore abounds. But all this is fast disappearing. The goat herds, the source of nature's lore, are almost a thing of the past, the old type of *vaquero* is fast becoming extinct, and the younger generation looks down with disdain on the old stories and traditions of its people. However, there are a few out-of-the-way *rancherías* along the border where the inhabitants still cling to their old customs and retain to a great extent *el amor a la tierruca*, dislike all innovations, distrust Americans and refuse to speak English. Thanks to these, a great deal of the fast-disappearing lore of the Texas Mexican may still be gathered. Most of the material here presented comes from three sources—the *vaqueros*, the *pastores*, and an old cook."

She further noted, "The stories of the *vaquero*, since he is in contact with people, are somewhat humorous, very human, and often realistic. On the other hand, the *pastor*, who lived alone in the pasture cut off from all intercourse with his fellowmen, produced mystical stories of the heavens, of birds and flowers and of other forms of nature. These are stories which he in solitary nights had woven and formed in his mind."

These sources of her works are the all-important bearers of precious news from our *pueblo*'s literary heart and soul of *aquel entonces*. Through her endeavors, González de Mireles claimed for us a poetic and inspired re-creation of our *pueblo*.

When she set out to collect folklore among the Texas-Mexicans of the borderlands, she was a young, single woman traveling by herself. She had heard some of the stories and songs she collected since her childhood; however, it took university training and, we are told, the urging of folklorist J. Frank Dobie to prompt her return to the borderlands to carry out her mission.

In 1927, when she was twenty-four, González de Mireles published her first efforts in the Texas Folklore Society's *Texas and Southwestern Lore*. Thus, she began a career that would see her ascend in 1931, at the age of twenty-eight, to the presidency of the Texas Folklore Society. She was the first Texas-Mexican to hold this post.

Her status as a single woman carrying out such trailblazing work was distinctly unique. She recalled in 1983 that when she conducted her research for her 1930 master's thesis, "Social Life in Cameron, Starr, and Zapata Counties," she took great care to defer to the tenets of a patriarchal society. She kept her hair long, solicited a letter of introduction from the archbishop of San Antonio, and knitted as she interviewed her subjects. González de Mireles understood that, despite her intellectual prowess and a Rockefeller Foundation grant, in her appearance and conduct she had to assure the *pueblo* that she was "*una persona decente.*"

By bowing to these demands for modesty and conservative attire and behavior, González de Mireles, with her knitting needles as well as her reference books, met patriarchal requirements with dignity and grace. She thus might be entrusted with the *pueblo*'s stories. One imagines that on her subsequent folklore research journeys she also packed those crucial *abujas* to gain entrée to the sites where *cuentos sabrosos* were in residence. Thus, no harm would visit a man relating tales to a woman diffidently bent over a complex knitting pattern, while politely extracting his stories "El Paisano," "The Mockingbird," and "The Devil on the Border."

Perhaps more important to recollect and honor is one undeniable truth: her folklore-gathering encounters netted rich, unself-conscious portraits of Texas-Mexican life. She attained such enduring treasures because she so wholly captured the spirit and soul of Texas-Mexican creative oral expression. Her folkloric representations contain themes that form the cornerstone of contemporary Chicano literature.

The work González de Mireles carried out engaged both the internal and external landscape that Texas-Mexicans made and in which they lived. She truly documented the Tejano *pueblo*'s understanding of the birds and the land; their mores and values; and a universe imbued with the people's poetic vigor and voice. This Tejano construction of reality and fantasy was the soul of the folklore she collected.

Her discourse calls us to believe that the white feathers of mocking-birds, the proliferation of ghosts, the tragedy of lost Spanish riches, or the wisdom of the village fool all arise from a fully formed Tejano cosmos that originated long ago, when, as she reported, all creatures spoke in Spanish. This universe was thus populated with humans, beasts, and a nature that teach us about life as only art can—and in a Texas-Mexican context. Moreover, the stories she collected were grounded in an ethnic sensibility and incorporated quite distinct gender roles.

Her remarkable efforts recorded the humorous, mystical, and real-istic stories born in, and nurtured by, the Tejano *pueblo*. As a folklorist, González de Mireles knew that she needed to save our *pueblo*'s unique stories. As a writer, she realized that only those *canciones* and *cuentos* that are permanently inscribed in black ink on white paper are remembered.

The extraordinary work of Jovita Gonález de Mireles secured our *pueblo*'s collective imagination, memory, and literature for all time. This is her legacy to us.

Women from Separate Corners of the Room

Forging a Collaborative Pathway to Tejana History

I begin with my poem "In the season of change," whose final line, "women from separate corners of the room," is echoed in the title and subject of this essay.

"In the season of change"

If E. Dickinson and I had been friends,
we would each have owned a treasure chest
filled with doilies for laying under our silverware,
for showing off atop our china cabinets.
For softening the scars in the 300-year-old dining room tables
we both would have inherited
from our great-grandmothers.

But our *bisabuelas* never met,
exchanged glances, or
sat next to each other in church.
And I only discovered E. Dickinson
in the few pages she was allowed
to enter in my high school literature texts.

Only years later did
I finally pore over her words,
believing that
her songs held
my name inscribed within.
And that they might fill the air

with the ancient signs of kinship
that women can choose to pass along.

And thus left on our own,
E. Dickinson and I
sat down at the same table,
savoring her rhubarb pie and my *cafecito*,
chatting and *chismeando*
and trading secrets
despite decrees demanding silence between us:
women from separate corners of the room.

"In the season of change" is about an imagined encounter between an unnamed Tejana poet and the nineteenth-century New England poet Emily Dickinson. In writing the poem, I envisioned their meeting as a delightful and fruitful exchange between equals who ignored the lies, the myths, indeed all the barricades set up to falsely separate one from the other.

In this essay, I suggest that in writing *Las Tejanas: 300 Years of History*, Ruthe Winegarten and I, women from separate corners of the room of Texas History, came together in a similar way at the turn of the twenty-first century to relate a fuller history of Spanish-Mexican women: *las Tejanas.*

In the Beginning

In mid-March 2000, Ruthe and I first talked about working together on a general history about Tejanas. Shortly before, we had seen each other in Austin at the annual meeting of the Texas State Historical Association (TSHA), where I took part in a panel on Tejana history Ruthe had organized.

My presentation was about the four Tejanas I had spent late 1999 and early 2000 interviewing for an oral history project. All four women—Sabina Palomo Acosta (my mother), Lucía Alderete Anaya (a second cousin), María Quiroz de León (a distant relative through marriage), and Juanita Palomo Campos (my maternal aunt)—lived all or most of their lives in the Central Texas Blacklands, where I was born and reared.

When I interviewed them, I had no idea that their oral histories would ultimately become the heart of a chapter in *Las Tejanas*: "Life in Rural Texas: 1900–1940."

After returning to Waco, Texas, I was in touch with Ruthe, telling her that I would likely move back to Austin by May or June 2000. She immediately offered to rent me an apartment attached to the back of her home. I remember that she described the apartment as "small but elegant." Over a couple more telephone conversations, Ruthe expressed great eagerness in my assisting with the history she and Dr. Yolanda Leyva Chávez planned to write about Tejanas. Would I, Ruthe asked, help them several hours a week in exchange for a very generous reduction in rent? Since I have the habit of agreeing to interesting opportunities, sight unseen, I told her I would be very pleased to help with the book and live in the apartment.

I subsequently made another trip down to Austin to inspect my new abode. At some point between seeing it and moving back to the city, I became the coauthor of the book because I consented to another of Ruthe's requests for assistance. One day, she informed me that Yolanda needed to devote her time to another commitment and was withdrawing from the project. Ruthe added that she would not write the book without a Tejana collaborator. Then, scarcely pausing, she asked me to step in as coauthor. Standing with the telephone to my ear in my apartment in Waco, I think I pondered her request for only a few seconds. Intuitively, I knew that if I spent too long thinking about undertaking such a daunting project, I would never agree to it. I also sensed that if I said no, perhaps this much-needed book on Tejanas would remain only a great idea for many years to come. So I said yes.

Later, I laughed at my audacity and perhaps my foolishness for agreeing to be coauthor. After all, I had only learned weeks before about Ruthe's plan to work on a general history about Tejanas that would span three hundred years. At the time, I shivered at the thought of anyone embarking on what had to be a very challenging endeavor. Now I had agreed to coauthor the book.

I moved into the apartment in the back of Ruthe's home in Austin on the last weekend of April 2000. Her office was located between my place and her living accommodations in her home. About two weeks later, on or about May 15, 2000, I sat down in front of a ten-year-old laptop donated to me for the project and started to work on the manuscript that became *Las Tejanas: 300 Years of History*. I did so without giving much thought to what the word "collaboration" meant.

Laboring Willingly

I had gained some limited experience in collaboration as a member of the research team for the *New Handbook of Texas* at the TSHA. This collaboration had generally been pleasant and rewarding but of brief duration. This was different; this was a book. Possibly up to two years of working intensely with someone else loomed ahead. Still, I put aside any doubts I might harbor about working with Ruthe. Indeed, I considered what our collaboration meant only after our book was published because several individuals asked me what it was like to write a book with another person. Embedded in their question was their own interest in having such an experience, coupled with their fear of having to give up power over their most cherished ideas to accomplish such a mission.

Their inquiries elicited other questions: How do individuals work as a team? How do they decide what their roles will be? What issues of control and power arise? How do they settle differences of opinion and perspective? Are they doomed to engage in a war of words and pettiness? Can their work ultimately be engaging, joyful, and successful? All these issues have forced me to reflect on the collaborative process that took Ruthe and me from the beginning to the end of our journey, with a manuscript we both liked in hand.

Two Women, Many Tasks

Ruthe made it clear from our first conversation after I returned to Austin that she preferred that I write the bulk of the manuscript and reshape all of it, including reworking her chapters through all the revisions. The book needed to have one voice, she believed. As it turned out, our manuscript of more than five hundred pages went through three complete revisions, and numerous mini-revisions of chapter subsections, prior to our submitting it to the University of Texas Press in early June 2001. Later we spent an additional fifteen months answering queries and doing minor revisions, based on the astute suggestions of our manuscript readers and superb copy editor, Letitia Blalock.

When I joined Ruthe on the book project in May 2000, she was already at work on the first chapter of the book. She agreed to work on other early history chapters, while I began the chapter that became "Revolution, Racism, and Resistance: 1900–1940" and would write the subsequent chapters through the end of the book. She also said that she would devote herself to acquiring the bulk of the illustrations. Moreover, we agreed that she would begin to draft the "Timeline" and the "Fifty Notable Tejanas" sections and begin to assemble the bibliography. Later we labored together intensely on these three parts of the book. During our many moments of exhaustion from overwork, we regretted having made a commitment to the "Timeline" since it required so much careful attention. In the end, we were very glad to have included it, as doing so provided a valuable shorthand guide to Tejana history.

The Composing Road We Took

At Ruthe's suggestion, I reviewed the outlines for the book she and Yolanda had drawn up. As we worked, we occasionally referred to them, but we also created our own plan. We also decided that each chapter should be written in small thematic sections that would allow reading the book with great ease.

In doing our work, we fell into a pattern: Ruthe organized the files containing materials we hoped to include in each chapter. She handed them over to me, and I would then devote the next several weeks to writing the chapter. Moreover, we were faithful to our joint agreement that I should draft one chapter per month and hand it over immediately to Ruthe for her review. We also sent some chapter drafts to individuals we trusted to provide us their frank assessments and suggestions.

Saturday Breakfast: Angst y Dále Gas

We quickly learned that having breakfast together on Saturdays was the best, most delicious, and least stressful way to talk to each other about manuscript problems we encountered. Most importantly, our Saturday breakfast visits moved us forward in thinking and writing as a team. Sitting at Ruthe's dining table, and occasionally at the long worktable in her office, we talked about the difficulties we encountered. For example, we were concerned that we did not have available one major source regarding Tejanas in business or the professions. This was a daunting hurdle to overcome because we were committed to including a chapter we had already entitled "Entering Business and the Professions." The evidence that Tejanas were business and professional women existed, but how we would discuss their entry into these areas was a major challenge.

To deal with this critical issue, we turned to the work on Tejanas that historians Cynthia Orozco, María Cristina García, I, and others had produced for the *New Handbook of Texas*. Moreover, we consulted Ruthe's voluminous files on Tejanas, collected over more than twenty-five years. Included in these rich sources was specific information on individuals, organizations, and companies that helped us dissect and consider what it meant to be a Tejana entrepreneur or professional. Fortunately, these materials, often the products of women's intellectual enterprise, served as our key guides in writing this chapter.

Although our difficulties with this chapter were particularly troublesome, we encountered a variety of similar challenges in writing the entire book. Our Saturday breakfast visits thus allowed us the time to share concerns, commiserate over problems, and, most importantly, plan a strategy to confront obstacles we faced. I prefer to call our Saturday breakfast strategy planning "*dále gas.*" The term, literally translated, means "give it some gas." The closest English approximation to "*dále gas*" might be "just do it."

Growing up in McGregor, Texas, I often heard my parents and neighbors invoke the term "*dále gas*" when the recalcitrant engine of a car refused to start. "*¡Dále gas!*" they enthusiastically shouted to the driver forlornly sitting behind the steering wheel. If all went well, the car would start, and off the driver would go. Ruthe and I invoked "*dále gas*" as our mantra in forging ahead on our important project.

Forging Our Collaborative Pathway

As we began our collaboration, I, like many others working in such an arrangement, was prepared to cling ferociously to my ideas, only to have Ruthe disarm me by insisting that I needed to have the final word about what appeared in the book. The authority I undertook as the "final word" was not, however, a merciless axe that I brandished to demolish anything about the book I did not like. In fact, my having the final word meant something quite the opposite to me. I saw it as an instrument with one specific goal: to shine the probing light of justice on stereotypes regarding Tejanas that might be found in our work. My charge was to examine and toss back into the sea of debunked Texas history patently false or questionable "facts" about Tejanas. These "facts" included anything that Ruthe or I might have discovered and collected in our files, suggested for inclusion, or wrote in the chapters unknowingly or naively.

I do not wish to suggest that Ruthe was deferring to personal proclivities and sensitivities I might harbor about Tejana history. Instead, from her point of view, my having the final word was necessary to produce a book that was as full and truthful an account of Tejanas as we could write.

As I worked with our massive collection of materials, reviewing and revising our efforts, I found little of deep concern. True, I spotted occasional words, phrases, or sentences that needed clarification, but that was to be expected as we tried to make our way as writers. I also refrained from actually considering myself the final word on all matters regarding Tejanas. I certainly could not then, nor can I now, consider myself the ultimate authority on my Spanish-Mexican progenitors. As I worked on the manuscript, I found it necessary to return to this cautionary advice to myself.

Certainly, my holding veto power over our manuscript seems to contradict the spirit of collaboration and to violate the collegiality that presumably governs the people involved: the commitment to listen to each other and to refrain from the temptation to wrest away the other's gifts and talents as a person, as a thinker, and as a writer.

Yet such a set of circumstances did not arise between us because, like the unnamed Tejana poet and the New England poet Emily Dickinson of "In the season of change," we were forging a new path, one where a Tejana was an equal and, as an equal, could be the leader.

Let me elaborate. Like many people born and reared in Texas, Ruthe's and my individual and group identities were shaped in a state whose history is littered with falsities or half-truths about Texas-Mexicans. As a result, we were both educated in an environment where obstinate reluctance to allow Tejanas a voice in our state's history was a common thread running through the state's official cultural and historical institutions.

It was over such treacherous terrain that we women from separate corners of the room traveled to our writing table. Thus, our adherence to my role as the "final word" in our project was perhaps the most genuine way to bring balance to a first-ever effort to place three hundred years of Tejana history on more intellectually honest ground.

I used my authority as the opportunity to heed the voices of my Spanish-Mexican forbearers as much as my collaborator's. Indeed, as I listened to my Tejana ancestors' voices, I was overwhelmed by the scale of their stories, through which they proclaimed their values, beliefs, and actions; confidently stated their own truths; protested what they had been denied; and resisted burdens placed upon them.

In hearing them out, I sought to understand how some Tejanas had been relegated to silence by circumstances beyond their power, while others had remained quite vocal despite efforts to silence them. As a result, I was duty-bound to let their stories guide me and to share my authority as the final word with the countless numbers of women whose lives filled the important Texas history we were writing.

Thus armed, I chose to carry the essence of their writings, speeches, poems, manifestos, and *testimonios* back to the table where Ruthe and I were attempting to write a Tejana history worth reading. Making my journey to our writing table was the true test of my having the final word.

When I think back on our many months of work, I am certain that I could not have written this book alone. I could have written my account, and Ruthe could have written her account. However, to write our account of *Las Tejanas: 300 Years of History*, we had to forge a collaborative pathway. In the end, we arrived there, all the while:

> chatting and *chismeando*
> and trading secrets
> despite decrees demanding silence between us:
> women from separate corners of the room.

Escritoras Tejanas

Sirviendo la Gente / Tejana Writers Serving the People

I begin with the words of United Farm Workers Union cofounder Dolores Huerta: "Every moment is . . . a chance to change the world."

Indeed, Spanish-Mexican women writers in Texas, women I call Tejanas, have produced works that are efforts to "change the world" for the better. Here I weave together three stories: how Tejana writers serve their people, how Elena Zamora O'Shea exemplifies this vision, and how Tejano professor John Morán González illustrates Zamora O'Shea's leadership as a writer through *El Mesquite: A Story of the Early Spanish Settlements Between the Nueces and the Rio Grande*, on the eve of the Texas Centennial of 1936. This book was first published in 1935 by the Mathis Publishing Company of Dallas.

In her introduction to *El Mesquite*, Zamora O'Shea wrote: "From my earliest childhood I remember the open country between the Nueces River and the Rio Grande; that vast expanse of territory that our early historians do not mention in the days of early history. Sometimes I have wondered why it is that our forefathers who helped with their money, their supplies, and their own energies have been entirely forgotten. History should be told as a fact, pleasant or unpleasant." (Zamora O'Shea, introduction to *El Mesquite*, unnumbered page).

Zamora O'Shea's words provide insights into how Tejana novelists, memoirists, historians, and poets serve our people through their deliberative, creative, and truth-seeking roles. In their works, we find generation-wide unity. As women of Spanish-Mexican origin, they are deeply aware of their multiple layers of racial and ethnic heritages. They also acknowledge a history lived in a geographic space replete with conflicts over land and social and economic values.

When I began to etch poems in the quiet of my home in McGregor, the Central Texas rural town where I grew up, I thought that no one among my people had ever put pencil to paper to write about us. It would be many years before I found out differently, and many, many more before I learned that I had a literary *abuela* named Elena Zamora O'Shea; she had been plowing the writing fields long before I was born.

In time, I discovered that Tejana writers had long before my birth begun to lead our people into the light of self-understanding and self-respect. These writers accomplished this feat by creating works from within the Tejana hearth. Such a commitment required an authentic engagement with their inner and exterior lives. From such a steadfast position, they became advocates for our people.

Zamora O'Shea arose from a group of twentieth century Tejana writers I call *las cuatro*. In addition to her, the others were Jovita González de Mireles, Fermina Guerra, and Emilia Schunior Ramírez. Separately and together, *las cuatro* were principal players during the early-to-mid-twentieth century, putting on paper genuine accounts of our people.

Las cuatro possessed three attributes in common: they completed college, they were educators, and they "wrote a whole body of history and folklore of the nineteenth-century Tejano ranching frontier." Historian Andrés Tijerina has noted that "they wrote with a powerful commitment to preserving the nobility of the Tejano ranch community values." Sadly, although *las cuatro* were deeply knowledgeable about, and united in their commitment to our community, they likely never met one another. (Tijerina, introduction to Zamora O'Shea, *El Mesquite*, xx)

Zamora O'Shea, much like Jovita González, came from a landed family. She was born on July 21, 1880, on Rancho La Cardeneña, which was located on her father's land grant in Hidalgo County. However, she was reared at La Trinidad, her mother's land grant at La Posta del Palo Alto. This ranch was "named for the stage coach stop La Posta," situated next to a tall tree known as El Palo Alto. This site is key to *El Mesquite* and to Zamora O'Shea's perspectives in relating our people's experience in settling Texas. (Zamora O'Shea, *El Mesquite*, xv, xvi)

She studied at the Ursaline Convent in Laredo, a boarding school. By the age of fifteen, she was teaching Mexican children at Palito Blanco, "a ranch school near Alice in Jim Wells County." Zamora O'Shea then studied at the Holding Institute in Laredo, the University of Texas, the University of Mexico, and the normal school in Saltillo, Coahuila,

Mexico. She received her teaching credentials from Southwest Texas Normal School in San Marcos. (Zamora O'Shea, *El Mesquite*, xvii)

When her long teaching career ended, Zamora O'Shea turned to writing. In approximately 1929, she commenced her documentation of Texas-Mexican "history in the Nueces Strip," using her father's papers and oral histories passed down to her by Doña Concepción García de Moreno, her maternal grandmother. (Leticia M. Garza-Falcón, introduction to Zamora O'Shea, *El Mesquite*, xxvii; John Morán González, *Border Renaissance*, 84, 86)

In *El Mesquite*, Zamora O'Shea introduces us to the ordinary day-to-day experiences, the cultural values, and the history of our people's early settlements. In doing so, she hands us an important key to unlock the door of greater knowledge about our community's claim to Texas. In this, her best-known contribution to Mexican American literature, Zamora O'Shea imprints the experiences of her family and other early Texas-Mexican settlers, whose ranches were steeped in our people's customs and traditions. She recognized that this way of life needed to be preserved in writing for posterity. Her account is set down via a witness narrator—a mesquite tree—that is key to the Tejano ranch, and thus to the Tejano community. That she chose such a narrator is a significant acknowledgment that the Tejano community is deeply connected to the land.

Zamora O'Shea tells us very early in her novella that ranch life required fortitude and initiative: "The ranches were far apart, sometimes twenty and thirty miles between settlements. The rancher and his family depended on themselves for support, entertainment, and aid." She provides numerous details on the family's nutrition: "Among the vegetables [available] were found yellow and red tomatoes, . . . pumpkins, [and] squashes. . . . Some of these vegetables are still grown by our people, who far from medical centers depend on themselves for medical aid." Zamora O'Shea also informs us: "For meats they had beef, mutton, lamb, hog, and chickens. . . . The women made butter . . . and cheese in abundance. . . . One of the old women served as midwife, and home doctor. Their ailments were few, living such clean lives as they did. I do not exaggerate when I say that the first man I ever saw intoxicated was when I went to the city to attend school." (Zamora O'Shea, introduction to *El Mesquite*, unnumbered page)

She then pointedly introduces El Mesquite, her narrator: "I AM of the highest quality of Mesquites. There are three members of our family in the Southwest. The *Arrastrado*, or spreading after the fashion of a common rambler, which furnishes very small beans, and no shadows for beasts or mankind; the *Mesquite*, which grows to some height, furnishing abundant shade in the summer and food during drouths for beasts; and my kind, which the Spaniards, the first white men to recognize my quality, gave the name of '*Mesquite Rosillo*.' This was because my wood has a roan color, and is excellent for cabinet work."

Throughout her book, Zamora O'Shea captures the "details of daily life: songs, local plants and folk medicines, foods and recipes, *peone/ patrón* relations, and the distinctive Tejano ranch vocabulary." (*El Mesquite*, inside book jacket)

Chapter titles illuminate her efforts to set down significant details: "Plant and Animal Life of the Region"; "Settlers of El Ranchito—Now Corpus Christi"; "Wedding Bells"; and "Land of Contention Between Two Republics." In each of the book's eleven chapters Zamora O'Shea illustrates the richness of our people's existence. Indeed, by setting down everyday experiences, she brought to life a vibrant community that dealt ably with the economics of the day and practiced a spiritual life.

Zamora O'Shea's account, moreover, illustrates how deeply attuned she was to the role of nature in Tejano life. Indeed, her mesquite narrator follows the seasons, detailing the specific roles of the inhabitants and visitors in the land surrounding the Tejano ranches. El Mesquite informs us: "The robins have passed on their way to the north. The geese have been gone some time. Now my summer birds are coming back and they will again sing to me and to all the countryside. . . . The ground all about is covered with tiny blades of grass. The Fathers [Catholic priests] stopped last night and slept under me." (Zamora O'Shea, *El Mesquite*, 11)

Summoning such images, Zamora O'Shea rightly becomes an early twentieth century American ecologist. This is important to note, since the literary depiction of American environmental consciousness has been deemed the province of white writers: Henry David Thoreau in the nineteenth century and Rachel Carson in the twentieth century.

Indeed, the author introduces the reader to a landscape enriched by the diverse life that inhabits it. El Mesquite states: "I am not alone any more in the vast open country. Several trees of different kinds have sprung up. Birds and horses are responsible for this. The mesquite seeds do not sprout unless they have passed through the stomach of animals. As the cow chews her cud, she does not disseminate seeds. But the horses pass many of my seeds unbroken and consequently they disseminate seeds everywhere. Birds bring from other sections seeds of berries they eat. In this way [many seeds] are spread from one section to another." She likewise teaches us about changes in Tejano living patterns: "One by one, the people left. Some went east to the settlements near the great sea, some went west to Casa Blanca, and some south to the ranchos near the Rio Bravo. (Zamora O'Shea, *El Mesquite*, 24, 34)

By setting down these details, Zamora O'Shea acts as both a creative writer and public servant, reminding us that the land where early Tejanos settled provided many riches and blessings. Just as importantly, she placed at the forefront a history that gave credence to a Texas-Mexican understanding of Texas. Her perspective grew especially notable as the celebration of the Texas Centennial drew near.

In *Border Renaissance: The Texas Centennial and the Emergence of Mexican American Literature*, John Morán González sheds light on Zamora O'Shea's bearing witness to the breadth and significance of Tejano history, one that insisted on public acknowledgment. She wrote: "Perhaps it is because so very [few] of the writers give the real founders of Texas, the Spanish colonists and Mexicans of Texas origin, any credit that I resent it. But knowing as I do that we gave Texas the Long Horns, the Mustangs, the tall tales adopted by the present generation . . . I believe it is the place of writers to give our section a slight bath in Spanish salts." (Zamora O'Shea in González, *Border Renaissance*, 67)

Chief among those Anglo-Texan notables Zamora O'Shea's novella disputed was her former student, the folklorist J. Frank Dobie. He had, by the time of the Texas Centennial, ascended to prominence, borrowing on the culture of Texas-Mexicans. Dobie was keen to celebrate the Texas Centennial by backing a project of 750 historical markers throughout Texas that granted prominence the Anglo-Texan claim to Texas history. The markers were, in fact, an imprecise historical account. González asserts that the markers attempted to wipe the state clean of Tejano, African American, or Native American existence, and touted Anglo domination over all other peoples or "obstacles." (González, *Border Renaissance*, 68)

The markers seemed akin to the well-known Anglocentric phrase refrain: "Remember the Alamo." This catchphrase did not acknowledge that the Alamo had long before existed as the religious site known as Misión San Antonio de Valero. Thus, into this world of 750 markers laying false claim to Anglo-Texan heroism arrived Zamora O'Shea, with her challenge to a spectacle that excluded our people. Her book, González states, set about "reclaiming Texas History" for Tejanos. (González, *Border Renaissance*, 67, 68)

To exemplify the deeply racist nature of the Texas Centennial that Dobie championed, González includes in *Border Renaissance* a photograph of Nazis involved in the celebration. Of their roles, he writes in the accompanying caption: "Myths of Nazi and Anglo-Texan racial supremacy converged at the Alamo in May 1935 as German sailors paid tribute to its Anglo-Texan defenders. Thus, in the Texas Centennial era, the Texas-Mexican defenders of the Alamo were erased from historical accounts of the siege and battle of 1836." (González, *Border Renaissance*, 30)

Further, González takes on Dobie's contradictory views regarding the value placed by Tejanos on the Texas landscape. On the one hand, Dobie wrote poetically about the beauty of the mesquite tree, the narrator of Zamora O'Shea's novella. He proclaimed, "The mesquite itself is a poem." Dobie, however, also condemned the tree that was as natural to Tejano life as it was troublesome to Anglo ranchers. "The mesquite has overspread itself. The machine age is meeting it," Dobie wrote in 1938. Dobie continued: "Ten-ton roller tractors . . . as formidable in appearance as any German war-tank, are to be found slaying the mesquite on the King, O'Connor and other ranches in southern Texas." And where the tractors failed, "ranchers waged merciless chemical warfare upon mesquites with root-killing kerosene." (Quoted in González, *Border Renaissance*, 79–80)

Dobie thus sought to make of the mesquite, however striking he found it, a pestilence that stood in the way of progress. Zamora O'Shea countered such a denigration; she embraced *el mesquite* for its beauty, its resilience, and its witness to the authentic Tejano ranch experience, thus to the Tejano people. Through her insistence on celebrating the enduring value of the mesquite, she refuted Dobie with a resounding nay. She returned to our people the "repressed memory of language and soil" and its importance to Tejano culture and history. "Combining the narrative modes of naturalist observation, oral storytelling, and social history," *El Mesquite* provided our people a means to understand who we were. (González, *Border Renaissance*, 80)

Doubtless, Zamora O'Shea's perspective was reinforced by her memory of teaching in Nueces and Jim Wells Counties. There she witnessed the "chilling effect" on her students of *A New History of Texas* by Anna J. Hardwicke Pennybacker. The book, first appearing in 1888, was an effort to disparage Texas-Mexicans. In correspondence with Tejano leader J. T. Canales, Zamora O'Shea recollected her students' response to *A New History*. She wrote, "I saw that all the children were stiff in their desks so I cut the lesson [on the Battle of Goliad] short." (González, *Border Renaissance*, 81, 83)

González informs us that Zamora O'Shea also took on Carlos Castañeda, who later became a renowned Tejano historian. At the time she contacted Castañeda, he was a librarian at the University of Texas, while studying for his doctorate there. In a letter to him, she protested that Pennybaker was weaving "falsehoods she passes off as history." Zamora O'Shea asserted: "Can't we descendants of the first settlers do something to stop the continual offenses against us in their history books? If they would study the true facts, and tell the truth, that would be fine. But they twist history so much that, according to them, our ancestors were truly brutish." She urged Castañeda, who had many archival records at his disposal, to lay out the truth from his more elevated place. In a letter to him dated October 20, 1929, she stated: "As you know, these matters must be proven with footnotes by historians." (González, *Border Renaissance*, 84–85)

At the same time, Zamora O'Shea feared that the official archives on early Tejano settlements were erroneous. Whereas Castañeda credited the records as truthfully stating that José de Escandón had "authorized" the first Spanish settlements in 1748, she informed him that long before that time, "people had already lived in those parts for many years." "Official history," she declared, "lagged far behind the movements of Mexican settlers." (González, *Border Renaissance*, 85–86)

Thus, Zamora O'Shea's *El Mesquite* is a work that depicts and memorializes for all time the "customs, occupations, and upbringing of our people." Indeed, her extraordinary work communicated the real toll, sacrifice, beauty, and joy in the lives of our Tejano antecedents, who chose to settle and to make their homes on the land that we know today as Texas. In her account, the *abuelas* and *abuelos* of today's Tejano community brought with them "a deep reservoir of cultural knowledge" and "the most modern ideas of general education and technological innovation." Moreover, Tejano ranchers deployed windmills long before Anglo-Texan ranchers, created schools to educate poor children, and committed themselves to passing along their heritage to future generations. (González, *Border Renaissance*, 86, 87, 89)

In writing *El Mesquite*, Zamora affirmed us and our history. Her great accomplishment in this significant work stands as genuine inspiration to the generations of Tejana writers who have followed her. United in spirit and knowledge, *escritoras Tejanas* carry on in creative service to the people.

Sources

González, John Morán. *Border Renaissance: The Texas Centennial and the Emergence of Mexican American Literature.* Austin: University of Texas Press, 2009.
O'Shea, Elena Zamora. *El Mesquite: A Story of the Early Spanish Settlements Between the Nueces and the Rio Grande.* College Station: Texas A&M University Press, 2000.

Act IV
Poems

(2013–2018)

2013
A reason to write a poem
Leaving all my clothing in Spain
Bashō
Patrolling the headways

2014
I abandoned my alarm clock
Quadruple dare
Sandwiched between yes and maybe
Safety is not
Sweet farewells
You will be completely healed
Let the past go
Finally, resting
Because I am no longer that person
Prepping
This morning at Mass
Disappearing

June 30, 2014
July 1, 2014
Last night I pledged myself anew
Doubtful no more
From here on
And on and on
On into the desert, I say
The time has come to tighten my belt
Nothing left to protect
One
Two
Three
Four
If I should venture
Looking for a way
Foreign
Karma
Although I could be wrong
Boxed or not
This one makes
The coming of September 2014
The last are the first

2015
Water
Make not haste
Gandhi not and yet
A small forest
Returning to poetry
Church
A ver
Faith: again
On the eve of the eve of Christmas
Rosal rojo, pinched, as usual

2016
Beginning yesterday
The world opens up

We must remember the dead before turning to the living
One book
March 9, 1949–2016
Day after
Grace, at least
Beginners mind: I
Beginner's mind: II
Perfectly imperfect
Imperfectly perfect
The things I have lost I have found again
Yesterday, Our Lady all dressed in white
Gathering flowers
Why, why not?
On the way to truth
The basics
Some days
Standing
Several turns around my prisoner's block
Bougainvillea

2017
Winter Mass
It's better
The red antique roses sway to and fro
Prepare
Skimming memoirs
Fear not
Florence: I
Florence: II
Florence: III
Florence: IV
Florence: V
Anti-sick series: I
Anti-sick series: II
Anti-sick series: III
Anti-sick series: IV
Anti-sick series: V
Cristobal

Diez y seis y contando
Company
Nine days and counting
Making ready the path

2018
Risk light
What if you die before you get to leave

August 8, 2013
A reason to write a poem

Why make a poem appear, if not to see
it curl into a vine going somewhere
ahead of us, seeking a cove to rest
its face. Then rise to give us back
our lives over coffee and conversation
to settle the world's problems.
At least our small circle of them: how the
lettuce in the burgers consumed at fast food
joints were pulled out of the dirt by Clara,
Esteban, Rico, Amelia: teens dreaming
of tree lines in the distances away from
these fields.

Poems are made for these wonderings
and for the shadows
lingering in the shade of cottonwoods.

So, I say shape and rearrange
everything in your life,
making it ripe for the giving.

August 19, 2013
Leaving all my clothing in Spain

I will fold my clothes
into a tiny bundle.

I will purchase two new pieces.
Maybe in Toledo, maybe in Madrid.
Maybe they shall be red or floral or black or blue.

At the end of my journey,
I will dress in one of them.
I will fold the other in my baggage.
Both will clothe me well enough
until my disquiet growls, wanting more.

Bashō

was said to travel lightly.

I embark with a shoulder bag,
a 3×4-inch notepad, and a pen,
eager to write down what I notice.

Bashō returned from one journey
poem-less.

Perhaps so shall I.

Patrolling the headways

of my yearlong sabbatical,
I come up short on wisdom gained
in the four and a half months
since its inception.

Many days I try to reignite
my once too active days,
measuring the steps that thwart
the new stillness and silence.
My patrols ask the perennial question:
Should I be or should I act
or should I act instead of be?

Pushing my brand-new broom across the stained
and perpetually dust-ridden hall
of my apartment building,
I try to sweep when I sweep,
to give each stroke its own house
in which to dwell in its own hour.

January 6, 2014
I abandoned my alarm clock

except to check the time
when I wake up in the middle of the night.
Up pops a light, declaring:
12:05 AM or 2:17 AM or 4:19 AM.

Some days my alarm-less clock life
becomes a prayer, teaching me to move slowly.
Some days
I do not know
how to impose myself less and less on myself.
How to find my way
toward whatever bread is offered
across the table from my companions.

January 20, 2014
Quadruple dare

A suitcase and a shoulder bag
filled with one pair of sturdy shoes
and three changes of clothing, sans
the toiletries that can be bought anywhere.

A year without anything else
but what fits in two bags,
lightweight of course.

Go, go, go.

Giving up a safe mooring
is the price of freedom.
Can I pay it?

Go, go, go.

Leave behind the fake passport
to the safe place
where nothing is ever safe.

Go, go, go into the storm.

January 21, 2014
Sandwiched between yes and maybe

the butterfly named faith forgives
my lack of resolve.
Forgetting my way,
I scurry up molehills of hope
and scurry down them just as quickly.
What evergreen caught my eye going up
is an obstacle on my descent.

I skid and slip and slide my way
along this sidewalk called
change now or forever be silent
about whatever pain I accepted
to be safe and secure:
24/7.

January 22, 2014
Safety is not

Safety has its problems in the long run,
I think of this
whenever it shows up as an option.

I know safety is good,
but it can weaken the gut,
the brain, the heart.

I like safety in bits and pieces,
when it does not interfere with
the poetry of a dog
with his butt sticking up, his front paws down,
his head up and his tail wagging,
in salutation to the woman walking him.

I like this kind of poetry
too much to cross the street

to escape the cold wind
of adventure blowing my way.

Safety, I give you up to
wander to the edge of the cracked sidewalk
where tree roots carved up its smooth passage
for hearts shaped by its gutted rocks.

January 27, 2014
Sweet farewells

We tend to send nicely scripted letters
with gentle words
to convey our sorrow at the pain
we have caused our beloved,
but we do not really mean
to vanquish their guilt
that they have let us go.

Years after offering our bogus forgiveness,
we troll through our pain and our loss,
finding this and that miserable thing to curse about
the idyllic landscape of our past,
the one before the breakdown.
Everyone laughs at our blindfold,
wrapped securely around our soul
and buckled down with chains.

It can take twenty years
before we figure our way
around the winding road filled
with the stones and thorns
of our betrayal,
our misery measured out
like copious portions of bad meals.
We circle the same streets,
looking for him or her or them, standing
under the streetlamp, waiting for us,
although it is long past the moment
to say goodbye and mean it.

March 21, 2014

You will be completely healed

For a reason known only
to the Buddha,
now that you are 65,
now that you are supposed
to begin to drag yourself around,
holding on to this and that chair and bannister,
to another's arm as you rise from a chair,
you will be completely healed.

For a reason known only
to God, you take up your cloak and go forth
without regretting what you have lost,
what lies in an unopened letter,
bidding you to wander into storehouses
others have invented for you to open.

For a reason known only
to your mother and father
as they ascended to another life
beyond the one on earth, you will be healed.
They are laughing about your aches,
your trips to multiple doctors,
the drugs prescribed
that did not alleviate your pain.
They are laughing about the two decades
it took you to discover
that your bank account has gone missing
dozens of hundred-dollar bills, seeking a cure.

For a reason that only God
and the Buddha, and 'amá and 'apá know,
you will be healed.
You will not live regretting
that you have not done what you thought
you were supposed to do
by the age of 24, 35, 50, and 65.

For a reason beyond all reasons,
you will be completely healed
and walk into the desert
that holds all the water you need,
and all the succulent fruits thriving
there for you.

For a reason known only
to you,
your faith will save you,
if you want it to.

April 21, 2014

Let the past go

A girl unheard
of before 2013 resides some streets away from me,
having arrived in the middle of the year:
she lives,
unmindful of real and imagined hurts.

She simply lives.

She will wait
until we are safely across the bridge of sorrow
before bringing us dozens of roses,
with their thorns intact,
their blossoms
in buds and full-blown blooms:
red, yellow, white, pink.

I see the giggles forming
at the sides of her lips,
as she curls her fingers around the roses.

What stories will we tell her?

Surely, she deserves beautiful words to decipher.
Especially those that resound with joy.
It is not my task to wag my finger at her

over past imagined pains and hurts.
It is only mine to pray that
she will wander through life,
filled with songs.

April 22, 2014
Finally, resting

After nine months,
the time to arrive at full term,
my heart has grown a centimeter.
It is barely an accomplishment.
Yet here it is,
raising its head
and a flag of surrender to a love
imprinted with psalms.

May 3, 2014
Because I am no longer that person

I have jumped ship
and made my way to another harbor.

I hear the birds' morning songs.
They invite me to
rest in the waters of peaceful surrender.

For this journey
I take prayers
I have memorized:
Catholic, Buddhist, poetic tithes.

I have set myself free from you.

I have journeyed beyond that place
where we crossed the same road map
into the agelessness
of the roads that lay before me,

spreading a timeless harmony,
like honey upon toast,
with eggs, papaya, or mango,
with the dearest of friends
gathered at the table and clasped to the heart.

May 8, 2014
Prepping

Ten months into this gestation,
I sit and sit, stand and stand,
type and type about
what awaits she who waits patiently
at the door,
wondering if this has been the right decision:
the one to wait a little longer.

What courage might I conjure
to breathe my life in and out,
taking a small change of clothing,
a map or two inside my head,
a few guides inside my heart.

Prepping will take so much more
than sitting or typing or standing
to learn how to widen the door
I must walk through on my way.

May 8, 2014
This morning at Mass

I found the sanctuary too austere.
I imagined in its place
a simple outdoor altar
surrounded by barrels of wildflowers,
no sirens going off outside.

June 20, 2014

Disappearing

from sidewalks,
from the errands we were running
to the grocery, to the drugstore,
strikes us with fear.

The neighbor who waves to us every day
wonders why he hasn't seen us in a few days.
He knocks on our door.
Hours later
the cops appear and break down the door,
only to find everything intact.

But I am talking
of another kind of disappearing:
the going into a life lived
above the timberline of distractions,
into a room big enough
for a straight back chair to sit upon and pray:
wordlessly, with or without a religion,
or with all the saints near us,
in whatever form we are called.
To disappear and
reappear intact below the timberline.

June 30, 2014

Almost July, one day 'til, in fact,
and then, what?
It seems to me that
I have been waiting for July 1, 2014,
for more than a month,
thinking all the while that
it will mean my deliverance
from a feeling of drudgery
on those days
when lifting one foot and then

the other seems too heavy a chore
for my sixty-five years of age.

But mainly I have been waiting for July 1, 2014,
to wave *adios*
to my staid existence amid fig trees,
sweet though they are: raw or baked into bread.

July 1, 2014

beckons with the strains of desert songs rising
from cacti
and the thorns of life pricking my limbs awake.

July 1, 2014
Last night I pledged myself anew

to a year of living frugally.
I do not know if that means
to step lightly in consuming food and drink.
In proclaiming my ideas, in abandoning my prejudices,
in backing off from defending either.
Or if I must enter
the unruly life of humility,
that I may learn the real necessities of life.

July 3, 2014
Doubtful no more

on the Feast of St. Thomas,
the choice to live
with the opening bud of faith attends to me
at the 8 AM mass.
The anointing of the day begins
with today's Gospel,
in which Thomas is said to demand
something along the lines:
Unless I see and unless I touch,
I shall not believe.

And then, of course,
he gets to see and to touch.

In the pews,
we murmur against Thomas,
doubter, doubter, doubter, doubter.
We sigh. We would never do such a thing
to such a holy man as Jesus.

But Fr. René tells us
our deepest doubts are no roadblock for
the bud of faith to bloom.
Or at least I think he said that.
Maybe I fell asleep
during this part of his short homily
or maybe I sat entranced
with the deep red of his vestment.

A doubting St. Thomas am I as well,
filled with a desire
to see the smallest
of my red rosebush's buds bloom and be fragrant.
And to touch and smell them.

July 9, 2014
From here on

nothing is as apparent
as that which
sets itself in front of me,
waving its hand back and forth,
to and fro, side to side,
asking "yoo-hoo, can't you see me?"

I woke up and knew immediately
that you had left
to venture across the unknown terrain
you had not yet explored:
love drawn

from some whimsy that grabbed you.
A love you wanted and there it was:
landing in your life.

I woke up and knew.

Although it broke my heart,
I was glad to know.
After all, I had written
in the church's community prayer book
that you should find a mate.
Of course, I prayed for a good one.
So, I asked the angel
who brought me the good news
in my morning bed
if she were the right one for you.
By and by you will know was the only reply.

Then I knew I would get on the road
to find contentment in mint tea.
In a toasted bagel eaten slowly.
In a stroll with deep friends
down shaded streets,
wishing all love would be as perfect
as these sweet moments.

July 15, 2014
And on and on

The petals on the sidewalk are scattered slips
of orange and lavender
blown farther and farther away
from the vines and trees
where they first bloomed.
They pause for moments
before the wind forces them
into graveyards down the street,
where no one will see
their original intention

to give us
their orange and lavender scents
upon swaying vines.

Quite by accident,
I looked down and saw the
orange and lavender petals,
one color saluting the other
and falling into its place.

I moved on, leaving the petals at rest.

When I wander this way again,
they will
have been driven on
by the wind,
or left to dry on the sidewalk.
Underfoot, they will be trampled by
the many shoes walking past that do not see them
as hands reach for cell phones to take
selfies of dried, pale faces
in August's high noon.

July 21, 2014
On into the desert, I say

To whatever place I embark,
it must be one
where I see the sun overhead,
during the hottest part of the day,
even when I complain about the heat.

There is no other way to stand in the desert,
no other way to see its life unfold.

On into the desert, I must go
despite whatever fears grip me,
on my uncertain journey, longing
for an easy route.

I will not forget the direction
I mean to travel this year.
I will not lose my way across a terrain
that points me toward
next year, with its flag of redemption
being stitched this year
by hands that caress desert winds.

July 24, 2014
The time has come to tighten my belt

We say we must tighten our belt
whenever we wish ourselves
into the neverland of consuming less food.
We announce it to ourselves
in front of our mirrors
and sometimes confess
our desire to others,
hoping
our public sharing will keep us honest.

But I need to tighten up my belt
in other ways
that are keeping me imprisoned.
I need to lessen the Internet's hold on me
as if I were some crazed lover
or an infatuated nut.
And so too the news
I have been reading on the Internet,
like a schoolgirl dutifully doing homework
that I no longer need to complete,
having perfected my score.

No more! I want to shout. No more.
I want to release myself
for at least a year from these peccadillos
the way I did from owning a job.

July 25, 2014
Nothing left to protect

Ten years on, and
between $1,500 and $1,600 spent,
I finally gave up my renter's insurance.

I had nothing left to protect,
not that there ever was,
except for a computer.
Not that it would be worth much
after depreciation.

Without fretting,
I let all that protection drain away
like sweat after a good walk,
with its multitude of deserved beads
filling every pore of my body.

The insurance representative on the phone
was polite but concerned
with my lack of protection
should an act of God befall me.
Still, she let me go
without questioning my judgment.
A $4 refund would be coming my way soon,
she assured me. (It never did.)

July 28, 2014
One

Ah, to contemplate
the act of losing
and then regaining the chance
to redeem myself.
Yes, indeed,
like the branches filled once more with berries.

July 28, 2014
Two

But if I hurry to make a choice,
what then?
I must stand still and straight and at ease:
not worrying
over planning a strategy
except that which wills itself
in prayer, mightily offered
like the psalms crying out for release
from the fire burning too much
of the soul away from its core.

July 28, 2014
Three

Upon third reflection is the way
to travel the road to deciding
how to use time, money, prayer.
The third time is the charm,
and all that, as the cliché promises.
Like the treasure buried in the field,
awaiting the eager and faithful servant,
her head crowned
in glorious flowers
that bloomed
only
because
of the gardener's patient tending
and waiting.

July 28, 2014

Four

Another time
I would have forked over my money right away
and left without any change
or even a nice pair
of pants and a blouse as a memory.
Another day
I would have paid off the bill collector
and run far, far away.
Another year
I would have put a down payment
on a machine neither necessary
nor anything I understood.

But that was then.

July 29, 2014

If I should venture

out to see the world
beyond the landscape
I encounter on my little periscope each day,
what would I find
along the hillsides and valleys?
The smooth plains? The knotty roads?

A blast of fresh air drifts toward me,
lifts the ends of my hair.
It casts a new light around me and calls me forth:
be not afraid of taking the wrong turn.

July 29, 2014

Looking for a way

I enter looking for poems
that are set outside the people and places
I have always known,
outside
the overly familiar territorial maps.

Where is the exit
that takes me far beyond my harbor?

Show me, I exhort my soul, and I will enter.

July 29, 2014

Foreign

Anywhere beyond the freeway
could pass as a foreign place
that I have crisscrossed going here and there,
high above the birds,
thinking myself sophisticated,
frowning on those
who have not ventured thusly,
hesitating over the costs and distances
and the strange foods.

But, truly, most terrains are foreign to me,
for I have lived as a hermit in a cell,
hidden away from contact with others unlike me,
fearing encounters
over anything
not resembling coffee and tea,
or bagels or muffins and scones
on mornings after Mass.

I must learn to sit
the way my mother did in any chair
she was offered,

exulting in whatever food was put in front of her,
hands raised over them, in hallelujahs,
blessing the pastry shop bakers
and the coffee farmers thousands of miles away.

I must-learn to sit the way Abuelo did,
as he exulted in the first bread I baked.
"*Haz mas, m'ija.*"

August 1, 2014
Karma

I should do away with
guesses and superstitions,
about why my life turned out as it did or did not.

In my midnight inventions,
when sleep comes and goes according
to its own whims, I mark
a new opening in the way ahead.
I will remember it the morning after,
when I decide that midnight wanderings
may be the true way out of cowardice,
out of an unwillingness to inch forward,
bearing both cross and holy water:
suffering and redemption united against angst.

August 5, 2014
Although I could be wrong

I will not worry if the parenthesis came
before the period
or if the bookends held the books in place,
collapsed to a side, or fell from the bookcase.

It doesn't matter anymore
if I am wrong
so long as I raise my voice,

whatever tinny sound it makes,
when I need to say
why I am opposed to people refusing to believe
in the legitimacy of a single verb cohabiting
with a single subject and a single object
and a single adjective in whatever order makes it bloom
the way a daffodil might:
    I bring yellow gems.
    I lay them here.
    I give them to you.
    Is this okay with you?
    I hope so.
My words sing better
than my gardening forays.
I imagine springs rising from their promise.

August 11, 2014
Boxed or not

The place they want you to occupy
gets smaller and smaller.

From your perch inside,
you sit all scrunched up,
your knees up against your chin,
your shoulders hunched over your chest,
your head tightly in between your thighs,
your nose breathing in your sweat,
breathing out your sweat.

And this is the way they want you to operate:
to tie yourself into a big wad of discarded
rolled up paper and be stuffed inside
for mailing to undisclosed destinations,
where you will surely die.

But no, no, no, no.

You are all open air and spinning curves
moving across a street at your own pace.

On your morning walk, you hear birdcalls,
the change in your pockets
calling you to buy a bit of yogurt.

I tell you, sisters and brothers,
escape from that box.

Believe me once, believe me twice.

August 15, 2014
This one makes

the umpteenth time
I have promised myself not to overindulge
or over-divulge or over-anything.
But I have not learned my lesson.

So it's back to the beginning,
the perennial square one,
where a hammer and nails
await my un-nimble hands.

And back to the first page,
where, again,
like a monk,
I begin anew every day.

Re-tasting the silence
and the jackhammer outside
and the weed eater
trimming blades of grass on a regular schedule,
as I learn to sit still amid
the noise out there and the noise inside.

The two combined are my carriage,
bearing me toward
the only nirvana I may know
so that on the umpteenth time

the noise may gradually fade
as I ascend the mountain roads
into new territories.

August 21, 2014
The coming of September 2014

will allow for recalibrating.
I will rid myself of my cooking forays.
I will eat what I eat when I eat it
and no more and no less and be happy.

I will buy only small helpings
and no more and no less and be happy.

What do I need
but some slices of this and that.
A water. A tea.

I will walk here and there,
gleefully chewing a piece of this
and that scone and savoring it
for the time it lingers to nurture me.

I am done with worrying
about its nutritional value.
I am done with worrying
about the wonders of carrots and spinach,
though I love them and will eat them.
I am sixty-five, after all,
an elder.
I shall wander here and there,
harvesting
my freedom to graze.

August 25, 2014
The last are the first

(with thanks to the Reverend Al Sharpton)
 The Reverend said,
preaching about the young man lost to bullets
careening through his body,
that another preacher,
needing rest for the coming sermon,
had sneaked
a preview of the ending
to the could-not-put-down-novel
and had learned what we already knew
about what happens to the first
in the wisdom stories the world over.

Oh, yes, that the first shall be last,
left holding the empty bag into which lies
have been piled,
one on top of another in our unforgiving hearts.

Oh, yes, that the last shall be first
to drink the water
and to break the bread of life.

The rest of us shall have to sweat
a very long while in the hot ovens
of our hatred
before the communion cup is refilled.

February 2015
Water

I will swallow cup after cup into my body,
lifting the liquid doctor
to my lips, bidding it to wander
into the well beyond it that

helps me survive the mistake of forgetting
that a gradual ascent
is best,
the one I had intended to take,
the wise choice I cast aside in my haste.

February 2015
Make not haste

My journey begins
in steps that flow
one level to the next.

I plan to survive
to recount the glories
of the mountain city.

May 10, 2015
Gandhi not and yet

The reddish lipstick, the pink sunglasses,
the yellow, lilac, green, aqua, orange,
and pink markers do not fit
a certain ascetic tint
required for justice-seeking souls.
But my set piece will carry me
on my own salt walk to the sea,
then back and beyond
with Gandhi.

He opens a palm.
Out falls the cloth his loom distilled,
as my thread and needle do here,
meandering over the stitches in my socks.

May 11, 2015
A small forest

surrounds my 320-square-foot hiding spot,
where, in my confinement,
I try my hand at sketching
the green leafiness that
coaxes me to reject
all the things that ail me.

The green leafiness that
surrounds my hiding spot
bids me to walk, confident
that I will reach
the other side of the street,
with budding white flower vines
in my hands.
And me sighing at the soaring sky above,
forgetting that I only thought
I could not walk.

September 6, 2015
Returning to poetry

I imagine that
the words will arrive
like anticipated kisses
and plant
themselves
in me.
My heart and brain are waiting.

September 11, 2015
Church

Hail Mary,
full of grace,
the Lord be with me,
and from thy womb,
the grace of Christ
that the Gloria sung
in soaring melodies repeats.

Blessed art thou among all people
and blessed the fruit of thy love
loosed into the world.

Holy Mary, mother of God,
Pray I sing to you all my days.

Church, you are.

September 18, 2015
A ver

These days I pray the Hail Mary as I walk,
sometimes assuredly, sometimes haltingly,
my cane at the ready.
These days I am caught inside a web of
sleeping, not sleeping; headaches, no headaches.
Shaky body. Steady body.

What way? What way?

I walk, reciting:
May I be at ease.
May I practice love and compassion.
May I come to the end of my suffering.

September 25, 2015
Faith: again

Walk.
Joy.
Walk.
Joy.

From here to there.
From here to there.

Faith is chasing me
up and down sidewalks again,
pitching its song to me:
walk joy.
walk joy.

From here to there.
From here to there.

Amen.

December 23, 2015
On the eve of the eve of Christmas

I begin anew breathing,
breathing.

On the eve of the eve of Christmas
I let go my judgmental voice,
breathing,
breathing.

On the eve of the eve of Christmas
God's light begins to peek a tad,
breathing,
breathing.

On the eve of the eve of Christmas
I pledge my troth to begin breathing.

I inhale God's light. I exhale God's light.
On the eve of the eve of Christmas
I decide to be brave for a change.
I am breathing,
breathing
into
my new love of cliff edges
I will no longer fear.

Christmas 2015

Rosal rojo, pinched, as usual

from a rosebush not mine,
carry my dreams
with Juan Diego on his halting trip
to Guadalupe/Tonantzin.

Spreading out
the roses in front of her,
he bows in a church
that both honors and despises womankind.

Rosal rojo, pinched, as usual,
carry me on new legs,
to love everyone every day.

Rosal rojo, pinched as usual,
from a rosebush not mine,
unbend my back, uplift my feet,
throw off my cane,
unbind my heart.
Make me yours in the deep *rojo* you live
regardless of how ill, sad, weary, dizzy
I am.

January 12, 2016
Beginning yesterday

I took a breath
and reached for a nearby antique red rose
conveniently close by.
The three of us—breath, rose, me,
traversed the sidewalk of Avenue C,
counting the streets back
—42nd, 41st, 40th, 39th, 38th and 1/2.
Ahhhhhhh. Breathe the breath.
Take in antique rose scent.
Pace, pace, pace,
unhurriedly.

Nearing home,
the rose and breath keep me alive,
attuned to the road arising
in my broken heart, spelling:
love, joy, hope, peace.

February 4, 2016
The world opens up

I clamor less,
laughing instead of railing.
I try to forgive my legs,
which do not behave when I ask them to please help me.
In this way,
I find a new Teresa.

What is this creaking
that becomes the open door
I talked so boldly of entering
when my legs walked
more hither and more thither,
farther than I needed to go?
Oh, I had such plans,

believing that they required
only my legs to fulfill.

Ah, what a sorrowful thing to behold:
the light in me
could not be released
until I nearly fell.

February 14, 2016

We must remember the dead
before turning to the living

A, you have died,
far from your hearth,
far from your nine children,
far from your wife,
who is decked out
in a resplendent blue gown
in a photo of you together.

A, I was sad to hear
that you died so suddenly,
so far away from your kin.
It's not just because
I lost my brother Jesse suddenly and far away.
Oh, yes, that has something to do with it,
I admit.
The sword that cuts through the heart
when someone calls to tell you
they have bad news.
The body begins to cave into the fetal position.

A, you died on a ranch in the Texas desert.
I wonder if it has mountains about,
all rangy and dark at night
and lit up in the morning
or in the evening after a rain.
I wonder if snow accumulates on them.

A, I like to think
of you and I meeting
somewhere,
far from our usual hearths,
to sit with another one,
sharing a meal of my mother's recipe
of corn tortillas, frijoles,
some *carnita asada*.
You might want seconds or thirds.
We could talk opera
and you could tell
what you look for in a composer.

A, I am a Catholic,
although probably not your kind of Catholic,
so maybe not a real Catholic
as far as you think.
Still, we share some prayers in common:
like today's responsorial psalm,
which cries out: "Be with me, Lord,
when I am in trouble."

A, I beg forgiveness
for the nonstop news announcements
of your replacement,
for abandoning the mourning period
after your death in West Texas,
where you had traveled for succor.

A, "Be with me, Lord,
when I am in trouble."

February 24, 2016
One book

Hey, Harper, you knew how to tell a story.

But we're all greedy,
always begging for more cookies and cake.
And you weren't a baker,
needing more flour and sugar and the like
to keep people happy.

We all know that one thick corn tortilla,
split at the top where it puffs up
and filled with butter and honey will keep us.

And you keep us too:
writing your best words.
What else did people expect?
Why do people want you to tell
many more times
what we already know?

March 1, 2016
March 9, 1949–2016

Sixty-seven years ago you gave birth to me
on March 9, 1949,
when you were 35 years old.

You told me that the day was cold.
You told me that I arrived at 6 that morning.

Today in Austin,
it is after 8 PM,
and I am only now beginning to pray for you
in thanksgiving.

'Amá:
I owe you the quiet at home for writing.
And the dining room table for writing.

And your patience
for my writing time that you closely guarded.

'Amá, these past 14 months have been a storm,
striking at me from every point.
I do not recognize who I am:
my legs unsure,
my soul unsure,
my heart unsure.
Myself wobbly in every inch
of my body.
I do not know
how to emerge from all this
or when or in what shape
or to what future reason.

But I do believe
in the posted sign
outside a Catholic center,
urging a Lenten solace:
"Give up who you have been
for the sake of who you can become."

Tonight, I pray at 8:42 PM,
by my wayward alarm clock,
that what I have been matters,
and what I might become matters.

In eight days, I will reach 67 years.
Oh, where should I step and with what joy?
I hear you laugh as I write this.

March 10, 2016

Day after

My body bends and shakes
and then straightens,
aligning me to whatever is before me:
the kind cashier inquiring

which flavor of gelato
I have purchased: coconut, I reply.

In my mind,
the aligning works,
carries me out to the rental
despite the nagging headache fog
that descends on me these days.

I figure it's one
or both
of the meds
or my body acting out.
Or maybe not.

So now, the day after turning 67,
I try to recalibrate and go more slowly
into the good day.

I remember one of my mantras:
love, joy, laughter, and peace.

May it be so again and again.

March 16, 2016
Grace, at least

A reprieve presented itself,
instructing me: journey on the path
of love, joy, laughter, peace.
With these stones build your life.

Those little tissue paper hearts
that showed up on my bedroom floor,
just like that
hinted the same: journey on the path
of love, joy, laughter, peace.
With these stones build your life.

March 22, 2016
Beginner's mind: I

I begin each day:
breathe in, breathe out.

Ah, beginner's mind is mine.
Make it more so in the coming days,
O Buddha nature.
Make it more so.

I daydream that were I in India
my puny soul
might already be emptied of angst.

March 23, 2016
Beginner's mind: II

Ah, the taunting, the blaming, the accusations:
all pouring from my mouth without a bit of proof.

What to do:
Retreat into forgiveness wherever I find it.
Retrieve notes left on the accused's door.

Sneak around,
hiding from the sunlight.

Today, I inch my way
toward kindness,
without stealing a rose,
for a change, to soothe my arthritic heart.

March 26, 2016
Perfectly imperfect

I always thought I would have the last laugh—
ha-ha, and all of that.

But, at 65, a sudden almost-fall
to the left made me perfectly imperfect.
With renewed headaches and trembles
and shaky legs.

Ha-ha, and all of that.

Some days I can see
that imperfection has rewards
as I trod slowly on my wobbly legs
a few blocks a day
and take photos of flowers I have stolen.

Ha-ha, and all of that.

April 5, 2016
Imperfectly perfect

I work these days on the flowers
I have pilfered,
pressing and gluing them,
sometimes sewing them, onto paper.
Day in, day out, with rests in between,
to turn them into music.

They sing imperfectly
perfect harmonies of
radiance on the days
spent bemoaning
the whys of my brother's death, of my illness.

The flowers, imperfectly perfect in my hands
live upon a piece of paper
for others to divine their sanctity,
their proper role in our endless arguing
over the place beauty should occupy.

April 7, 2016

The things I have lost I have found again

Today, for instance,
it's the green gazing at me from a branch
along the sidewalk
I often traverse, blindly, it seems.

Ah, God,
you have given me again these things that I have lost:
my soul seeing
the many beauties singing in front of me.

Let me go down in sleep tonight in gratitude
and rise tomorrow in gratitude and live my life.

April 9, 2016

Yesterday, Our Lady all dressed in white

reigned at the
Holy Spirit Chapel
I once disdained
as resembling a gym.

She beckoned me.

My eyes lit on her before Mass.
Come up to me, she commanded.
Tell me what you need.

The young man who helped with communion
that day knelt in front of her after Mass,
then rose and touched Our Lady gently
and caressed
the white spray of flowers at her side.
He seemed to do both for me as well.

Heal me, *virgen*, I said.
Then I left.

April 13, 2016
Gathering flowers

off branches and vines in neighbors' yards.
One at a time, usually.
Sometimes two at a time.
An antique rose one day.
A primrose the next.
Then a lantana.
And on and on.

They are my jewels,
the real deal that men don't show up with
when you want them to:
these *cositas* plucked
or cut and stolen away
and hidden in a pocket
or brought home in broad daylight
without remorse.

I could give up most of my stuff
for daily glimpses of them in every season.
And for their scents
caressing the rest of my life.

I mostly live for seeing *flores naturales*
laid out in beds and bins and on the ground,
parading themselves
as matters of love in my life.

April 20, 2016
Why, why not?

Organize the shelves,
the few threads, the paper,
the ridiculous number of supplements
I might want to stop ingesting.

A laziness seeps in,
greeting a brain

without enough rest overnight,
wondering why, why not?

A haziness seeps across my eyes,
fomenting confusion
about what I need to keep,
to give up,
wondering why, why not?

But standing at the counter,
tapping away at the keyboard,
I know I can throw myself into the spring blooms
in my neighbors' yards.
Why not.

July 29, 2016

On the way to truth

There are hairpin turns
and traffic circles planted with
Pride of Barbados,
Rosemary, and Bougainvillea.
Colors and scents to force me to right myself.
To force me to pay attention.
This too is gardening.

July 29, 2016

The basics

You would know what I mean
if you buy only the basics too.

Underwear. Tops. Bottoms. Shoes.

And then there are
a few basic food groups I dare to eat.

Nothing more,
except that I can always think

of something else
my heart must fetch
for my feigned worldly happiness.

August 29, 2016
Some days

I am full of unrequested opinions, declarations,
suggestions, amendments, complaints.

Some days they drown out the fragrance
of the flowers down the street.

May my prayers take over.
and do a clean sweep.

September 30, 2016
Standing

In my poem,
the women are first imagined kneeling,
grinding corn,
which they did: both kneel and grind corn.

In my poem, the women are imagined
standing up,
standing up, standing up,
when they needed to, and they did.

In my poem, the women know
how to kneel and how to rise,
how each stance is theirs
to choose for the task at hand
on all their *metates*.

So, when I learn someone is afraid
of watching a woman fight evil,
I wonder why and what the problem is?
I am impatient with such a stance,

this refusing to stand up,
this continuing stance
of kneeling before evil.
It is not the way women behave.

Grow up is what we do in body, mind, spirit.

We take our minds and fill them
with tools to think.
We take our spirits and fill them
with the wings
of Monarch butterflies:
with their strength to fly and fly and fly
to reach their nesting ground.

At the ramparts,
a woman afraid
will get you killed in body, mind, spirit.

Grow up is what we do.

October 6, 2016

Several turns around my prisoner's block

can bring me into myself:
legs and mind, heart and soul, and, yes, nerves.
Ah, yes, they're declaring,
okay, girl, you are well,
you are well, you are well,
even if you are not well, believe me,
you are well enough, girl.
Go in there
and sit and wait on God to talk to you.

At least 15 minutes around the block and
I am beginning to wake up
to whatever God plans for me.

At least 30 minutes,

and that plan has a short paragraph of love
to dish out to me as the wind hits my face,
as the sun falls over my shoulders,
warming me for the coming foray
into territory God rules.

At least 45 minutes and
I am caught up staring down
a neighbor's flowers
or nabbing one from a bush
skirting another neighbor's yard.

When I turn around to return home,
I am turning around to go forward into
whatever plan is set out for me,
no matter how afraid of it I am.

October 12, 2016

Bougainvillea

You are love on fire,
overflowing your corner of the yard,
brimming with deep pink and plum.
You bring joy to me this morning
that I have chosen to walk
without a cane,
shaking and leaning a bit to my left side.

I continue like a gleeful fool.

You tell me to pack a light suitcase
and leave for parts unknown
with a knowing heart that will seek the sun.

February 25, 2017

Winter Mass

What wind is stirred
as I make my way
toward the succulent fruit
it offers?

Does God speak
only when men enter
in their vestments
in all the churches in the land
at precisely 9 AM?

I am hungry
for more
than the usual pronouncements
of the Gospel
from only certain lips.

I want to learn about
our earthly fruits and troubles
in a woman's voice and cadence.

I think of this on this winter night.

June 1, 2017

It's better

To sway and sashay
to "Bidi Bidi Bom Bom" and "Paloma Negra."

To gussy up in mariachi pants and *chaqueta*,
a flower in the hair.

To turn off the TV
and walk *el camino* that lies
just outside my rental.

To forget, to forgive.

To set free
the persistent insects
who regularly visit my shower stall.

June 7, 2017
The red antique roses sway to and fro

in humid 11 AM mornings.

A thief has stolen some brother petals
and dropped them one by one on the sidewalk.

There they lie, turning darker and darker.
Their lifeblood ebbing.

June 26, 2017
Prepare

to change,
move a millimeter in your mind each day.
Yes, measurements alter the day's lesson plan.
Twelve minutes increases by thirty seconds.
Then twelve minutes jump to thirteen.
Three times per day.

This is a practice for living
as if each step matters.

June 29, 2017
Skimming memoirs

I've no time to dwell
on tales wailing over
alcohol-laden childhoods

in Swiss Alps chateaus
or posh cabins in the Maine woods.

Flee from me, you sagas.
Send me the truth, and more,
on which to dine.

August 2, 2017

Fear not

because in the end, as in the beginning,
fear is poison we drink. It lathers
up and rinses itself inside the gut,
then settles into our heart.

Fear not, says our heart,
as it preps its muscles
in morning light.

August 6, 2017

Florence: I

A dream budding,
pink, yellow, mauve, green.
Its long branches spinning around
in the moist dirt scented with rain.

Oh, that I may yet see your hills, your sun.

August 7, 2017

Florence, II

Shall I climb your hills freely
to attempt a summit.

Inside me lives a tumult,
unworthy one moment,
exalted in the next.

How shall I break down the bricks
cemented against escape,
both real and imaginary?

August 8, 2017
Florence III

I shall adorn my hair before I arrive.
It will be tinged with grey,
the brown becoming less and less apparent
as 68 becomes 69 and then 70 years.
Will the Florence sun
show any of the red shades it once had?
Will the Florence sun
warm my hair with its light?

August 9, 2017
Florence IV

How does one walk there?
Constantly gazing up.
Or looking down.
Or gazing at the distance.

From afar, on a sheet of paper,
I linger and muse and wonder
about the good to be had there
as the day begins, proceeds, ends.

August 10, 2017
Florence V

The library books about you had nice titles,
some were very learned.

One book was extra heavy
when I lifted it.

The words in the book were heavier.

A dread set in immediately:
I was going to be lectured.

Oh, no, not about you,
with a name that begins with *flor*,
the Spanish for flower.

Oh, no, Florence,
I will not listen to that rabble,
imprisoning your scent
—*florecita* that you are.

September 4, 2017
Anti-sick series: I

Get up.
Yes, that's right. Get up.
No cave to hide in.
Yes, that's right.
Get up.
Walk from.
Walk away from.
Walk away to.
Yes, that's right.
Get up. Now.
No sorrow.
Yes, that's right.
Get up.

September 4, 2017
Anti-sick series: II

Antibiotics.
Anti-seizures.
Which to try?
And why?

Some takers will live.
Other takers will not.
And others will walk
into the night and paint.

September 5, 2017
Anti-sick series: III

To heal.
That is my answer to the query:
What ails you?
Doesn't matter say I.
I only need to offer up
my limbs, innards, and soul.
Soak them with grace.
All will be altered. Healed.
By and by.
In what some call "the fullness of time."

September 6, 2017
Anti-sick series: IV

The spirit matters, of course.
It is as holy
as plum blossoms.
Harvested on time.
Pruned as required.
Watered.
It endures,
though winter arrives.

September 7, 2017
Anti-sick series: V

A patient stands
in the tree asana
for 60 seconds.
first on one leg, then the other.

A patient watches the rising sun
or the gathering night.
The next moment ends in release.

Oh, make my life so.

October 9, 2017
Cristobal

What was your cause?
It's just,
you see,
that *indigena* truth
is eternally imbued
in the *tierra* where you landed.

October 9, 2017
Diez y seis y contando

Marchamos pa'ya, pa'cá,
enraging university professors and presidents.
Shut up is what their closed doors shouted.

We downed our *chocolate y pan dulce,*
warmed our hands, marched on.
¡Echale otra!, we yelled on the UT main mall
with its carved letters
insisting that the truth sets you free.

"Don't worry, Abuelo!" Maximo shouted:
Aqui vengo, accompañandolos.

October 11, 2017
Company

A chair.
A mat.
A chant.
A prayer.
A walk.

We sit
stand
kneel
lie down
rise
together.

This, my company and I, do every day.

October 19, 2017
Nine days and counting

Two suitcases full.
Maybe a box or two.
That's all. That's it.
What to leave out?
Whatever does not fit.

November 2, 2017
Making ready the path

Mami *y* daddy, bent at the waist,
grasp palm fronds.
They are sweeping, sweeping, sweeping
the road in front of their *casita*.

Come, Teresa, come Olivia,
come Jesse, come Andrés,
they say.
We are preparing the way for you.

We prance behind them,
Olivia, Jesse, and Andrés and me,
laughing, laughing, laughing.

I pull Olivia's hand,
who pulls Jesse's hand,
who pulls Andrés's hand.
We are running, running, running
on the path
they have swept for us to follow.

Their fronds remain fresh,
giving off the scent of roses.

Quickly, now, move ahead of us!
Mami *y* daddy shout.

March 29, 2018

Risk light

What if *la espíritu santa*
were the main thing
I packed in my traveling bag.
It could wheedle me into
being an overnighter—a la carte,
I would sojourn without a trace
of angst over things left undone,
unspoken.

May 14, 2018

What if you die before you get to leave

for the trip you have taken over and over
in your head?

There's always the correct answer.
You simply pack and leave
as the day emerges

with rain or sleet or snow
or with the sun out
and temperatures in the low 70s.

Up ahead you enter
a bridge far from
the days spent racing to doctors and tests
and warnings about making sure
you're here next year for the annual.

The chorus warning you will never let up,
unless you set your watch to now.

Alleluia.